THE BIG BOOK OF KiD SERMONS AND OBJECT TALKS

Gospel Light

How to Make Clean Copies from This Book

You may make copies of portions of this book with a clean conscience if

- you (or someone in your organization) are the original purchaser;

- you are using the copies you make for a noncommercial purpose (such as teaching or promoting your ministry) within your church or organization;

- you follow the instructions provided in this book.

However, it is ILLEGAL for you to make copies if

- you are using the material to promote, advertise or sell a product or service other than for ministry fund-raising;

- you are using the material in or on a product for sale; or

- you or your organization are **not** the original purchaser of this book.

By following these guidelines you help us keep our products affordable.

Thank you,

Gospel Light

Gospel Light

Editorial Staff: Publisher, William T. Greig

Senior Consulting Publisher, Dr. Elmer L. Towns

Publisher, Research, Planning and Development, Billie Baptiste

Managing Editor, Lynnette Pennings, M.A.

Senior Consulting Editors, Dr. Gary S. Greig, Wesley Haystead, M.S.Ed.

Senior Editor, Theological and Biblical Issues, Bayard Taylor, M.Div.

Editor, Sheryl Haystead

Editorial Team, Amanda Abbas, Mary Gross, Karen McGraw

Contributing Editors, Jay Bea Blair, Linda Mattia

Designer, Carolyn Henderson

Contents

Big Book of Kid Sermons and Object Talks

Object talks can draw children in and help them apply the Bible verse to their lives. These object talks can be used as children's sermons or used to supplement any Sunday School curriculum. They can also be used to augment any children's ministry program, day school or homeschool curriculum.

Getting the Most Out of an Object Talk

Preparation is the key to using the *Big Book of Kid Sermons and Object Talks!* Read a talk at least several days ahead to give ample time to gather the needed materials. You may find it helpful to practice some talks before presenting them.

Whenever possible, invite children to participate. Each week ask a different child to read the Bible verse aloud (highlight the verse in your Bible and mark its location with a bookmark).

Occasionally describe situations in which knowing God's Word has helped you. Tell children how the Bible verse presented in the lesson has been important to you.

Using an Object Talk During Adult Worship

If the children in your church are in the adult service during the first part of the service, consider using the object talk as the basis for a weekly children's sermon. Give the talk, and then if possible, ask one or more of the Discussion Questions found in bold print at the end of each talk.

Conclude

These metallic items followed their leader—the magnet. We can choose the kind of people or leaders we want to follow. God gives us people who can lead us to obey Him. Read Deuteronomy 6:18 aloud. **What does this verse say we should do?** Volunteer answers. **We all need leaders who will help us do what's right in God's eyes and obey Him.** Pray, thanking God for people who help us obey Him.

Bible Verse
"Do what is right and good in the Lord's sight, so that it may go well with you."
Deuteronomy 6:18

Discussion Questions
1. **What kind of people do we often think of as leaders?** (Teachers. Parents. Coaches.)
2. **What kind of people make the best leaders?** (People who will help us do what's right in God's eyes.)
3. **Who has helped you obey God?**
4. **Who is someone you can help obey God? What is a way you can help that person obey God?** (Pray with him or her. Show him or her a good example by obeying God.)

Helping Kids Make the Transition to Adult Worship

For a few moments, let's do a little pretending. Let's pretend that we are six-year-old children and that we are sitting in the adult worship service of our church. What words will we hear that we don't understand? What books are we asked to use that we don't know how to read? What happens in front that we can't see because we are small? What are we expected to do that is confusing to us? How long do we have to sit still when we are not used to sitting?

As you think through some of the things your children experience in a typical worship service, you may come to the realization that the adult worship service sometimes becomes an uncomfortable, passive experience for a child rather than an opportunity to praise and worship God.

However, you as a children's program leader, as well as parents, pastor and others involved in leading the adult worship service, CAN take many specific actions to make the service more meaningful and enjoyable for children. Whether the children in your church are approaching the first time they will attend the service, attend the service only occasionally, frequently attend at least part of the service or are about to be promoted from their own children's church program into regular attendance at the adult worship service, here are some specific suggestions to help them enjoy and benefit from being with the grown-ups in "Big Church."

When Children Are in the Worship Service

Encourage parents to sit with their children near the front of the worship service. They will not only see and hear better, but they will also have more of a sense that the person up front is speaking to them. Proximity encourages participation.

Arrange for those who are involved in leading worship to meet periodically with the children in fairly small groups. This can be done briefly at the end of Sunday School or as a part of another children's program. Use this time to explain one feature of the service the children are about to attend. If this is done every week or on some other regularly scheduled basis, the children can gradually be introduced to the entire spectrum of worship activities which occur in your services.

A significant bonus of this approach is that children will also get to know your leaders as friends who care about them, rather than viewing them as strangers who lead unfamiliar ceremonies at a distance. Perhaps of even greater significance, this brief time of interaction will alert these leaders to the presence of children in the worship service, helping the leaders become more effective in including children in the worship experiences.

HINT: If you invite someone to meet with the children and this person is not experienced in speaking at a child's level, structure the time as an interview which one of the children's teachers or leaders will conduct. Let your invited guest know ahead of time the specific questions that will be asked.

Provide parents with a sheet of tips of things to have the child do before, during and after the service in order to gain maximum understanding and participation.

Tips for Parents

Before the Service:

- Sit near the front where your child can easily see what is happening.
- If your church prints an order of service in the bulletin, help your child identify, find and mark locations of hymns and Scripture readings.
- Let your child underline all the words in the bulletin he or she can read.
- Briefly explain the meaning of any difficult words or phrases in at least the first hymn you will sing.
- Share your own feelings about the hymns or songs to be sung: "This is one of my favorites," "I really like to sing this because it helps me tell God I love Him," "This is one I've never learned—I hope it's easy to sing," etc.

During the Service:

- Let your child help hold the hymnal or song sheet. Run your finger beneath the words being sung to help your child follow along. If your church displays the words of each song on an overhead, make sure you sit where your child can see the words.
- Touch your child (not just when the wiggles are in action) to build a sense of warmth in being together.
- Provide writing and/or drawing materials. Encourage your child to write or draw about things he or she sees or hears during the service ("Draw a picture of something the pastor talks about in his sermon.").
- If there is a time of greeting one another, introduce your child to those around you.
- Let your child take part in passing the offering plate, registration cards or other items distributed throughout the congregation.

After the Service:

- Express your appreciation at being in church with the child.
- Commend your child for specific times when he or she was participating well ("You really did a good job singing that first hymn.").
- Talk about what went on in the service. Avoid making this sound like an exam, but ask one or two questions to let the child know that you expect him or her to be listening. A few good questions to use are "What is one thing you remember from the service?" "Which song did you like best?" "What Bible person did the pastor talk about?" and "What was the pastor trying to teach us about?"
- Share your own answers to those questions, or let your child ask you any questions he or she desires.
- Explain one or two things that happened in the service that you think your child was interested in or could have been confused by.

Tips for the Children's Program Leader

As the children's program leader, you can also take specific actions to make the adult worship service more meaningful to the child. Look at everything that is done through a "six-year-old's filter." Ask yourself, *What would a child understand from what we just did?* This is not a plea to conduct six-year-old-level worship services, but it will help adults become aware of children's presence and their right to be led in meaningful worship of the Lord. The child will not understand EVERYTHING that occurs in every service, but the child deserves to understand SOMETHING in every service.

Meet with the person(s) responsible for planning the worship service and talk about ways to make the service more helpful to children. Consider these ideas:

• Choose at least one hymn or song with a repeating chorus, which makes it easier for children to learn and participate.

• Choose at least one hymn or song with fairly simple words and melody.

• Introduce at least some hymns with a brief explanation for children.

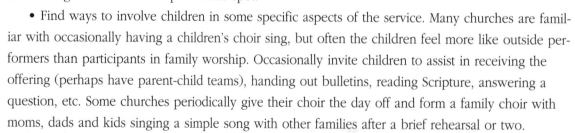

• Once or twice in the service mention, "Our children are worshiping with us and we want to help them know what we are singing (talking) about." This will help raise the congregation's awareness of their responsibility to guide children and will also explain some things to adults and teenagers that they might be embarrassed to ask about.

• Provide simple explanations of special observances (baptism, the Lord's Supper, etc.).

• When inviting people to greet one another, remind them to include children in their interaction. Instructions such as "Talk to at least one person from a generation other than your own" or "Greet someone who is now attending school" are enjoyable ways to alert adults without making the children feel put on the spot.

• Find ways to involve children in some specific aspects of the service. Many churches are familiar with occasionally having a children's choir sing, but often the children feel more like outside performers than participants in family worship. Occasionally invite children to assist in receiving the offering (perhaps have parent-child teams), handing out bulletins, reading Scripture, answering a question, etc. Some churches periodically give their choir the day off and form a family choir with moms, dads and kids singing a simple song with other families after a brief rehearsal or two.

• If the adults in your congregation wear name tags, provide name tags for the children, too.

• Provide clipboards, paper and crayons for children to use during the service. Before the sermon, the person leading the service can suggest that the children listen for a particular person or event during the sermon and draw a picture about that person or event on the paper. Children may pick up the clipboards during a hymn or some other appropriate time just before the sermon.

- Make a checklist of things for the children to listen for during the service. As the children hear one of the things listed, they check it off the list.

- Several months before children are promoted from their children's church program into regular attendance at the adult worship service, plan to have the children participate in a portion of each service each week or the entire service once a month.

- Ask a person with video equipment to make a recording of the entire worship service. Then, occasionally choose specific parts of the service to show and explain.

- If the order of worship is printed in your bulletin, give each child a bulletin and briefly explain the order of worship. Describe in childlike terms how each part of the service helps us worship God.

- If your congregation sings a song often (such as the "Doxology" or "Gloria Patri"), teach it to the children. You may also help them become familiar with the Lord's Prayer or the Apostles' Creed (if they are used in your church) by repeating them from time to time in your program.

- Help children understand that worship is anything we do that shows that we love and respect God. Use your conversation to help your children understand how praise, music, prayer and learning from God's Word are all important aspects of worship.

Leading a Child to Christ

One of the greatest privileges of serving in children's programs is to help children become members of God's family. Some children, especially those from Christian homes, may be ready to believe in Jesus Christ as their Savior earlier than others. Ask God to prepare the children to receive the good news about Jesus and prepare you to communicate effectively with them.

Talk individually with children. Something as important as a child's personal relationship with Jesus Christ can be handled more effectively one-on-one than in a group. A child needs to respond individually to the call of God's love. This response needs to be a genuine response to God—not because the child wants to please peers, parents or you, the leader.

Follow these basic steps in talking simply with children about how to become members of God's family. The evangelism booklet *God Loves You* is an effective guide to follow. Show the child what God says in His Word. Ask the questions suggested to encourage thinking and comprehending.

a. God wants you to become His child (see John 1:12). **Do you know why God wants you in His family?** (See 1 John 4:8.)

b. You and all the people in the world have done wrong things (see Romans 3:23). **The Bible word for doing wrong is "sin." What do you think should happen to us when we sin?** (See Romans 6:23.)

c. God loves you so much He sent His Son to die on the cross for your sins. Because Jesus never sinned, He is the only One who can take the punishment for your sins (see 1 Corinthians 15:3; 1 John 4:14). **The Bible tells us that God raised Jesus from the dead and that He is alive forever.**

d. Are you sorry for your sins? Do you believe Jesus died to be your Savior? If you do believe and you are sorry for your sins, God forgives all your sins (see 1 John 1:9).

When you talk to God, tell Him that you believe He gave His Son, Jesus Christ, to take your punishment. Also tell God you are sorry for your sins. Tell

Him that He is a great and wonderful God. It is easy to talk to God. He is ready to listen. What you are going to tell Him is something He has been waiting to hear.

e. The Bible says that when you believe in Jesus, God's Son, you receive God's gift of eternal life. This gift makes you a child of God. This means God is with you now and forever (see John 3:16).

Give your pastor the names of those who make decisions to become members of God's family. Encourage the child to tell his or her family about the decision. Children who make decisions need follow-up to help them grow in Christ.

NOTE: The Bible uses many terms and images to express the concept of salvation. Children often do not understand or may develop misconceptions about these terms, especially terms that are highly symbolic. (Remember the trouble Nicodemus, a respected teacher, had in trying to understand the meaning of being "born again"?) Many people talk with children about "asking Jesus into your heart." The literal-minded child is likely to develop strange ideas from the imagery of those words. The idea of being a child of God (see John 1:12) is perhaps the simplest portrayal the New Testament provides.

Quick Change

Listen to God your whole life.

Teacher Materials

Bible with bookmark at Exodus 15:26, stopwatch or watch with second hand.

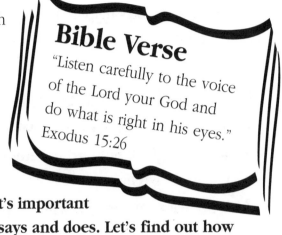

Bible Verse

"Listen carefully to the voice of the Lord your God and do what is right in his eyes."
Exodus 15:26

Introduce the Object Talk

Sometimes you might think that only grown-ups need to listen to God. But God wants everyone—for their whole lives—to listen to Him. When you listen to someone, it's important to pay careful attention to what the person says and does. Let's find out how good we are at paying attention.

Present the Object Talk

1. Ask children to look at you for 10 seconds, paying attention to the details of how you are dressed.

2. Ask children to close their eyes (or you may briefly step out of the room). Quickly change one detail about how you are dressed (remove glasses, take off a sweater, roll up sleeves, etc.).

3. Ask children to carefully look at you again, trying to identify the change you made. After change is identified or after 30 seconds, repeat activity with yourself or with volunteers. Vary the difficulty of changes made according to the age of children. As children are guessing changes, comment occasionally about the way in which they are paying careful attention.

Conclude

What does this verse say about listening and paying careful attention? Read Exodus 15:26 aloud. **Listening to God's voice helps us know how to love and obey Him. We can listen to God's voice as we read and hear Bible stories and as we pray to Him.** Lead children in prayer, asking God's help in listening to Him and doing what's right in His eyes.

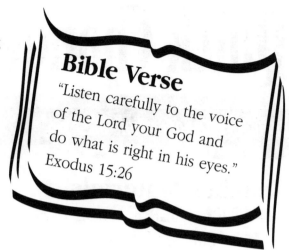

Bible Verse

"Listen carefully to the voice of the Lord your God and do what is right in his eyes."
Exodus 15:26

Discussion Questions

1. Who are some people you listen to?

2. When might it be hard to remember to listen to God? (When someone wants you to do wrong.)

3. Who are some people who help you listen to God?

4. How can you help others listen to God? (Pray for them. Talk with them about what you read in God's Word.)

Magnetic Leaders

Teacher Materials

Bible with bookmark at Deuteronomy 6:18, sheet of paper or card stock, magnet (toy magnet or refrigerator magnet), several iron or steel items (paper clips, nails, pins, washers, etc.).

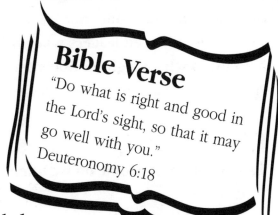

Bible Verse
"Do what is right and good in the Lord's sight, so that it may go well with you."
Deuteronomy 6:18

Introduce the Object Talk

The Bible talks about leaders, people who help others think and act in certain ways. God wants us to look for leaders who will help us do what's right in God's eyes. Look at the way in which these objects follow their leader.

Present the Object Talk

Hold paper or card stock horizontally. Invite a volunteer to experiment with the magnet and the items you have collected by placing an item on top of the paper and then moving the magnet under the paper to lead the item around on the paper. Repeat activity with other volunteers and items.

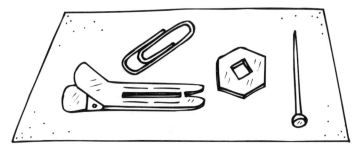

Conclude

These metallic items followed their leader—the magnet. We can choose the kind of people or leaders we want to follow. God gives us people who can lead us to obey Him. Read Deuteronomy 6:18 aloud. **What does this verse say we should do?** Volunteer answers. **We all need leaders who will help us do what's right in God's eyes and obey Him.** Pray, thanking God for people who help us obey Him.

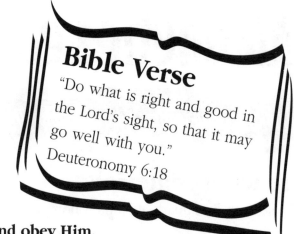

Bible Verse

"Do what is right and good in the Lord's sight, so that it may go well with you." Deuteronomy 6:18

Discussion Questions

1. **What kind of people do we often think of as leaders?** (Teachers. Parents. Coaches.)

2. **What kind of people make the best leaders?** (People who will help us do what's right in God's eyes.)

3. **Who has helped you obey God?**

4. **Who is someone you can help obey God? What is a way you can help that person obey God?** (Pray with him or her. Show him or her a good example by obeying God.)

Mission Impossible?

God encourages us when we're afraid.

Teacher Materials

Bible with Joshua 1:9 marked with a bookmark, 8½×11-inch (21.5×27.5-cm) paper, scissors.

Prepare the Object Talk

Practice cutting paper, following directions below.

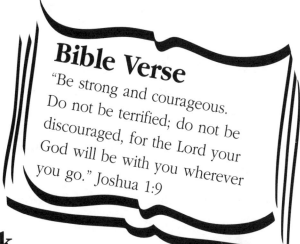

Bible Verse

"Be strong and courageous. Do not be terrified; do not be discouraged, for the Lord your God will be with you wherever you go." Joshua 1:9

Introduce the Object Talk

God gives us courage, even when we have something really hard to do. Look with me at this impossible task!

Present the Object Talk

1. Show paper and ask, **How might I fit my whole body through this paper?**

2. After children conclude that the task is impossible, fold the paper lengthwise. Cut the paper as shown in Sketch a, making an uneven number of cuts approximately ½ inch (1.25 cm) apart. Cut on the fold between the first and last sections as shown in Sketch b. Then carefully open up the folds and step through the circle you have made.

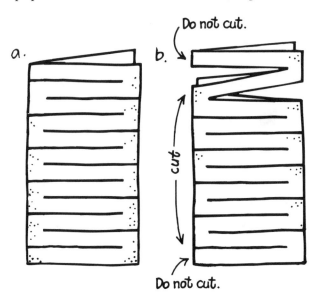

a.

b.

Do not cut.

cut

Do not cut.

Conclude

When something seems too hard to do or we're discouraged, God can help us by giving us courage and helping us know what to do. What does God promise to do? Read Joshua 1:9 aloud. Thank God for encouraging us when we're afraid.

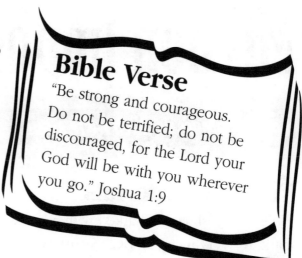

Bible Verse

"Be strong and courageous. Do not be terrified; do not be discouraged, for the Lord your God will be with you wherever you go." Joshua 1:9

Discussion Questions

1. **What might make a kid your age feel discouraged, or feel like giving up?**

2. **When is a time a kid your age might feel afraid and need to ask God for courage?**

3. **What are some ways in which God encourages us?** (Gives us friends and parents. Gives us promises of help in the Bible.)

Use Your Senses

Teacher Materials

Bible with bookmark at Job 12:13, blindfold, several small objects (quarter, eraser, walnut, plastic letter, etc.) in a bag; optional—one of each object for each group of six to eight children, bell.

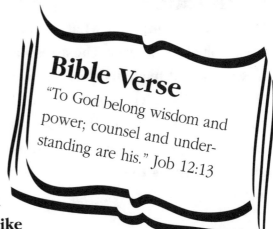

Bible Verse

"To God belong wisdom and power; counsel and understanding are his." Job 12:13

Introduce the Object Talk

The Bible tells us a lot about what God is like and why He is greater than anyone else. We're going to discover one way God shows that He is wiser and greater than anyone.

Present the Object Talk

Select several volunteers—one volunteer for each object. Blindfold the first volunteer, hand him or her an object and ask volunteer to identify the object. Repeat with each object, using a different volunteer.

Variation: Bring a variety of scents for volunteers to smell while blindfolded (orange peel, cotton ball sprinkled with vanilla flavoring, onion slice, etc.).

Small Group Option

1. Groups of six to eight children sit in circles, with their hands placed behind their backs.

2. Secretly give one child in each circle an (eraser).

3. Allow time for child to feel the object with his or her hands, trying to identify the object but keeping its identity a secret. At your signal, child passes the object behind his or her back to the next child in the circle, keeping the object hidden in his or her hands. (Optional: Ring bell as signal.) Continue process until all children have had an opportunity to feel the object. Then identify the object aloud. Repeat with a variety of objects.

Conclude

How did we figure out what each object was? Volunteers answer. **The awesome way in which God made us shows how great and wise He is. How does Job 12:13 describe God?** Read verse aloud. **The words "counsel" and "understanding" mean that God's knowledge is greater than anyone else's. Discovering how great God is helps us see why it's so important to obey Him and never think that our ideas are better than His.** Thank God for His wisdom and power.

Bible Verse

"To God belong wisdom and power; counsel and understanding are his." Job 12:13

Discussion Questions

1. **What are some other ways our sense of touch helps us?** (Tells us when something's too hot to eat. Lets us know when we need to wear a coat.)

2. **What other senses did God give us? How do they help us?** (Sense of smell helps us smell fire.) **How would our lives be different if we didn't have these senses?**

3. **What are some other ways we see God's greatness and wisdom?** (The way trees and flowers are made.)

4. **How can you obey this wise and great God?** (Be kind to others. Help friends. Be honest.)

Thumb Wrap!

Teacher Materials

Bible with bookmark at Psalm 95:6,7; masking tape; a variety of objects (pencil, paper, book, a cup of water, marker, paper clip).

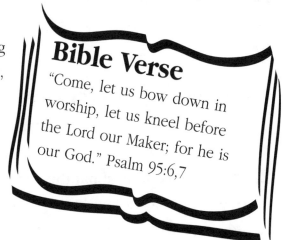

Bible Verse

"Come, let us bow down in worship, let us kneel before the Lord our Maker; for he is our God." Psalm 95:6,7

Introduce the Object Talk

Getting to know what God is like helps us believe in Him and worship Him. Try this experiment with me to learn about a special way God made us that shows His great power.

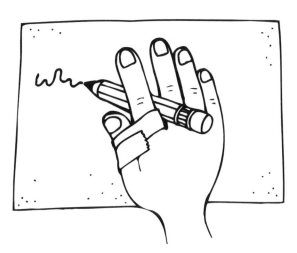

Present the Object Talk

1. With masking tape, wrap together the thumb and first finger of a volunteer's writing hand. Then ask the volunteer to try to write his or her name on a piece of paper.

2. Repeat with other volunteers and these tasks: turn pages of a book, drink cup of water, pick up a paper clip, open a door, button or unbutton a coat or sweater, etc.

3. Discuss the activity by asking, **What made your task so hard to do? What would happen if you didn't have a thumb? What would happen if you only had thumbs on your hands?** Volunteers tell ideas.

Conclude

God made our fingers and thumbs to work just right. Listen to these verses that talk about God as the One who made us. Read Psalm 95:6,7 aloud. **One way to worship God is by thanking Him for making us.** Lead children in prayer, thanking God for making us in such special ways.

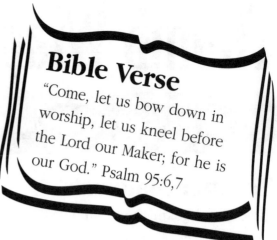

Bible Verse

"Come, let us bow down in worship, let us kneel before the Lord our Maker; for he is our God." Psalm 95:6,7

Discussion Questions

1. What are some other special ways that God has made us? (We can taste different flavors. Our arms and legs have joints, so they can bend.)

2. What's something about the way you're made for which you want to thank God? Tell children something you're glad God has made you able to do.

3. What are some of the ways people in our church thank and worship God? (Sing songs of praise. Pray. Tell others about God's greatness.)

Message Fun

Teacher Materials

Bible with bookmark at Psalm 105:1, paper, markers.

Prepare the Object Talk

On each sheet of paper, write one of the following personalized license-plate messages: "CRE8OR" ("Creator"), "GDLVSU" ("God loves you"), "GDS4EVR" ("God is forever"), "GD4GIVS" ("God forgives") and "GDSGR8" ("God is great").

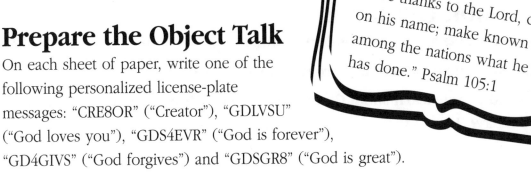

Bible Verse

"Give thanks to the Lord, call on his name; make known among the nations what he has done." Psalm 105:1

Introduce the Object Talk

Because we're glad to know about God and His love for us, we want others to know about Him, too. See what you can discover from these special messages.

Present the Object Talk

1. When have you seen a personalized license plate? Volunteers answer. **People get personalized license plates because the plates tell messages the people want others to know.**

2. Listen to this Bible verse to find out what messages we can tell. Read Psalm 105:1 aloud. **When we tell about the great and wonderful things God has done, we help others learn about Him.**

3. One at a time, show the license-plate messages you prepared. Allow volunteers time to discover what the message on each plate says.

(Optional: Give paper and markers to children for them to create additional messages about the great and wonderful things God has done, limiting messages to seven characters. Display papers in a well-traveled area of your church.)

Conclude

Lead children in prayer, inviting volunteers to name great and wonderful things God has done.

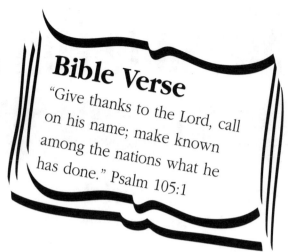

Bible Verse
"Give thanks to the Lord, call on his name; make known among the nations what he has done." Psalm 105:1

Discussion Questions

1. What are some great and wonderful things God has done?

2. Who has told you about how great God is? When?

3. How did people learn about God in Bible times? How do people learn about God today? (Listen to others who tell about God. Read His Word.)

Never-Ending Love

Teacher Materials

Bible with Psalm 117:2 marked with a bookmark, two 12×2-inch (30×5-cm) strips of paper, scissors, tape.

Introduce the Object Talk

God's love and His faithfulness last forever. Something that lasts forever has no end. Let's make something that doesn't have an end or a beginning—and gets bigger and bigger.

Bible Verse
"For great is his love toward us, and the faithfulness of the Lord endures forever." Psalm 117:2

Present the Object Talk

1. Hold up two strips of paper. **Where's the beginning of these strips? the end?**

2. Tape strips together at one end to make one long strip. Flip one end of the strip over (see sketch a) and tape it to the other end, so paper loop has a twist. Make sure joined ends are completely covered with tape.

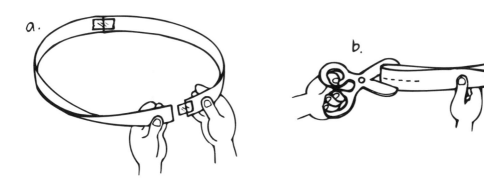

3. Fold strip and cut down the middle of the loop (see sketch b). (Loop will expand to double size.) Cut down the middle of the loops at least one more time.

Small Group Option

Prepare two strips for each child to tape together. Child will then cut the loop at your direction.

Bible Verse

"For great is his love toward us, and the faithfulness of the Lord endures forever."
Psalm 117:2

Conclude

Now our paper strips have become a big loop which has no beginning or end. What does Psalm 117:2 say lasts forever? Read Psalm 117:2 aloud. **"Faithfulness" means always keeping your promises and doing what you say you will do. God is faithful and His promises last forever.** Thank God for keeping His promises.

Discussion Questions

1. What are some things other than God's love and faithfulness that don't seem to have a beginning or end? (Sky. Ocean.)

2. What are some of God's promises to us? (Always hear our prayers. Always help us. Never leave us.)

3. When might someone your age need to remember one of these promises?

Mirror Talk

Teacher Materials

Bible with bookmark at Psalm 118:6,7; one or more hand mirrors; paper on which you have printed the sentence "The Lord is with me" backwards (see sketch).

Materials for Children

Paper, pencils.

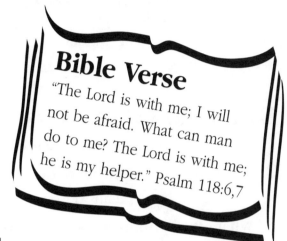

Bible Verse

"The Lord is with me; I will not be afraid. What can man do to me? The Lord is with me; he is my helper." Psalm 118:6,7

Introduce the Object Talk

Because He promises to be with us, God can help us even when we're worried or afraid. Look at these words and see if you can figure out what they say and how God helps us in difficult times.

Present the Object Talk

1. In class, show words you printed to one or more volunteers and ask them to try to read the words. **How hard is it to read these words? Why don't they make sense when you first look at them?**

2. Hold words up to a mirror and invite several volunteers to read the words. Volunteers write sentence backwards and use mirrors to read words.

Conclude

Sometimes we might feel like all the wrong things are happening to us. We might feel like we can't understand why sad things happen to us or to others. But if we remember that God is with us, we can ask Him to help us know what to do. Read Psalm 118:6,7 aloud. Thank God for promising to be with us even in difficult times.

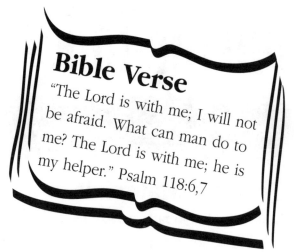

Bible Verse

"The Lord is with me; I will not be afraid. What can man do to me? The Lord is with me; he is my helper." Psalm 118:6,7

Discussion Questions

1. When is a time kids your age might feel afraid or worried?

2. What are some of the ways God helps us? (Gives us parents and friends. Promises to hear and answer our prayers.)

3. What other promises does God give us? (To forgive us when we do wrong. To give us courage.)

Seek and Find!

Teacher Materials

Bible with Psalm 119:2 marked with a book-mark, blindfold.

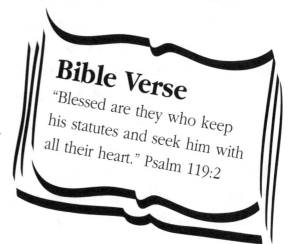

Bible Verse
"Blessed are they who keep his statutes and seek him with all their heart." Psalm 119:2

Introduce the Object Talk

We follow God's instructions because He knows the best way for us to live. But sometimes things make it hard to follow instructions. Watch to see what happens when we make it hard to follow instructions.

Present the Object Talk

Invite a volunteer to wear a blindfold. Then instruct the volunteer to complete a task such as one of the following: walk to the table across the room and pick up the

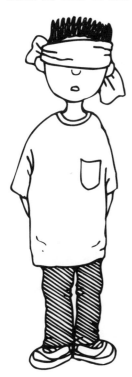

Bible, find the chalk and write your name on the chalkboard or play a music tape in the cassette player. Repeat with other volunteers and additional tasks. Occasionally ask volunteers, **What would make it easier to find what you're looking for? If you really wanted to do what I asked you to do, what would make it easier?** (Take off the blindfold.)

Conclude

Wearing a blindfold makes it difficult to find what you're looking for. Ignoring or disobeying God's instructions is like wearing a blindfold, and it gets us into lots of trouble. Listen to Psalm 119:2 to find what happens to people who learn about and follow God's instructions. Read verse aloud. **"Statutes" is another word for God's instructions. When we seek or try to follow God's instructions, we can find the best way to live.** Thank God for His instructions and ask His help in following them.

Bible Verse

"Blessed are they who keep his statutes and seek him with all their heart." Psalm 119:2

Discussion Questions

1. **What are ways kids your age might be tempted to disobey God? What might be the results? What kind of trouble might happen?**

2. **Why is it so important to God that we obey His commands?** (He loves us so much, He wants us to have the good things that result from obeying Him.)

3. **When can you obey God?**

Stronger Than Sin

Knowing God's Word will help us when we are tempted.

Teacher Materials

Bible with bookmark at Psalm 119:11, one or more bottles of vitamins (if you have very young children, you might want to bring empty vitamin bottles, child-proof bottles or empty bottles).

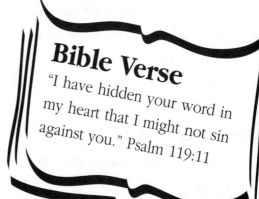

Bible Verse

"I have hidden your word in my heart that I might not sin against you." Psalm 119:11

Introduce the Object Talk

One of the best ways God's Word helps us is when we're tempted to sin—to disobey God. God's Word helps us be strong and obey God. Let's talk about some things that can help us grow stronger.

Present the Object Talk

1. Show bottle(s) of vitamins. Invite volunteers to read aloud the name(s) of the vitamins. **Why do people take vitamins? How might taking vitamins or eating foods with lots of vitamins help us?** (Helps us stay healthy. Helps our bodies grow strong.)

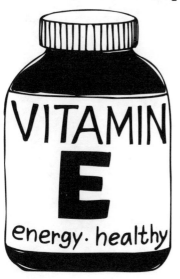

2. One at a time, pantomime (or ask an older child to pantomime) these actions: lifting weights, jogging, getting enough rest, drinking water. Children guess each action. **All these actions can help us become healthier and stronger.**

Conclude

The Bible tells us about something we can do to help us be strong in our desire to obey God when we feel like doing wrong. Read Psalm 119:11 aloud. **What does this verse say we should do to keep from sinning? What do you think it means to hide God's Word in our hearts?** (Read and think about God's Word. Memorize it.) Lead children in prayer, thanking God for His Word and asking His help in obeying it.

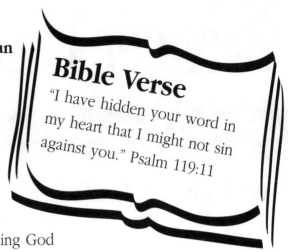

Bible Verse

"I have hidden your word in my heart that I might not sin against you." Psalm 119:11

Discussion Questions

1. **When are some times kids your age might be tempted to do something wrong?**

2. **What can we do when we feel like disobeying God?** (Remember the right things God's Word says to do. Ask God for help in obeying Him.)

3. **What are some other ways God helps us obey Him?** (Gives us parents and teachers to help us learn about Him. Promises to answer our prayers. Promises to always be with us. Helps us remember verses from His Word.)

Who's First?

We show our faithfulness to God by making good choices.

Teacher Materials

Bible with Psalm 119:30 marked with a bookmark, coin, two straws or paper strips of different lengths, baseball bat or stick.

Bible Verse

"I have chosen the way of truth; I have set my heart on your laws." Psalm 119:30

Introduce the Object Talk

Every day we make many choices—what we're going to wear and what we're going to eat. Some choices, however, are more important than others and show our faithfulness to God. Let's talk about some of the ways we make choices.

Present the Object Talk

1. How do you and your friends choose who will take the first turn in a game? Volunteers answer.

2. Lead volunteers to take turns participating in one or more of these ways of choosing: *(a)* Toss a coin in the air. Two volunteers call heads or tails. *(b)* Hold straws or paper strips with lower end inside hand so that they appear to be the same length.

Two volunteers choose straws or paper strips to see which is the longest. *(c)* Beginning at one end of a bat or stick, two volunteers alternate grasping hold of the bat or stick to see whose hand is the last hand placed at the other end of the bat. *(d)* Choose a number between one and twenty. Two or more volunteers guess number. *(e)* Place hands behind back holding a coin in one hand. Two volunteers choose which hand they think holds the coin.

Conclude

These kinds of choices help us when we're playing games. But the Bible talks about the most important choice of all: whether or not we will be faithful to God. What does Psalm 119:30 say about this important choice? Read verse aloud. Choosing the way of truth means to choose to believe in and obey God. When we make good choices, we show that we want to love and obey God. Ask God for help in making good choices.

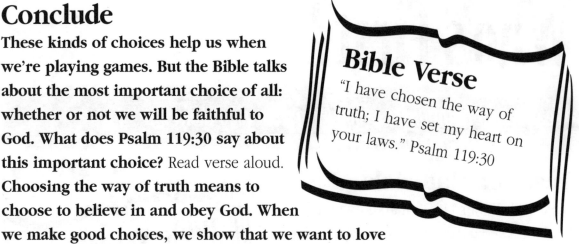

Bible Verse

"I have chosen the way of truth; I have set my heart on your laws." Psalm 119:30

Discussion Questions

1. **Who is someone you think makes good choices? Why?**

2. **What are some good choices kids your age can make at school? at home? How do these choices show love and obedience to God?**

3. **What might make it hard to make a good choice?** (When you want to do something else. When others might make fun of you.) **Who does God provide to help you make good choices and show faithfulness to God?** (Family. Friends. The Holy Spirit.)

Road Signs

Teacher Materials

Bible with bookmark at Psalm 119:59, separate sheets of paper on which you have drawn road signs (see sketch).

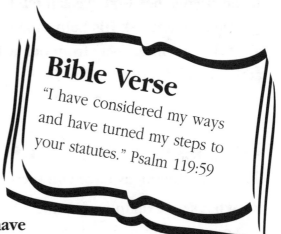

Bible Verse

"I have considered my ways and have turned my steps to your statutes." Psalm 119:59

Introduce the Object Talk

God wants us to think carefully about His commands and how we can obey them. Let's talk about what we can do when we have disobeyed God.

Present the Object Talk

1. One at a time, show each of the road signs you drew. **What would the driver of a car need to do to obey this sign?** Volunteers answer. Explain road signs as needed.

2. Which of these signs help us know what to do when we realize we have disobeyed God? Children tell ideas. **The stop sign reminds us that we should stop doing what's wrong. The U-turn sign tells us we should turn away from doing wrong and start doing what God says is right.**

Conclude

Read Psalm 119:59 aloud. **What word in this verse means the same as "commands"?** ("Statutes.") **Psalm 119:59 reminds us to choose to obey God's commands. None of us is perfect; but when we disobey God, we can tell God we're sorry and ask His help in making a U-turn—turning away from our wrong actions and doing what's right.** Pray, asking God for help in obeying Him and thanking Him for forgiving us when we sin.

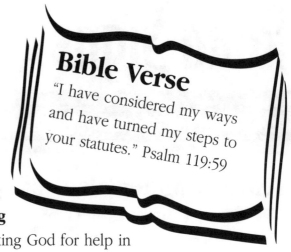

Bible Verse
"I have considered my ways and have turned my steps to your statutes." Psalm 119:59

Discussion Questions

1. **What other signs have you seen on the road?**

2. **What's an example of a time a kid your age might choose to stop doing something wrong and start doing something right?**

3. **When are times you are tempted to disobey God?**

4. **Who can help you obey God instead of disobeying Him?** (God promises to help us obey. God gives us parents, teachers and friends to help us obey.)

Timed Tasks

Teacher Materials

Bible with bookmark at Psalm 119:60, stopwatch or watch with second hand.

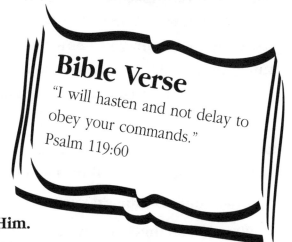

Bible Verse

"I will hasten and not delay to obey your commands."
Psalm 119:60

Introduce the Object Talk

When someone tells us what to do, sometimes we obey right away and sometimes we put off obeying. God wants us to be ready and quick to obey Him. Let's see how quickly you can do what I say.

Present the Object Talk

1. Hold up your watch. **What are some of the things we use watches for? How do watches help us?** Volunteers respond (tell what time it is, get to places on time, bake a cake, play the right number of minutes in a game, etc.).

2. Sometimes people use watches to find out how fast they can do things. Invite volunteers to take turns completing one or more of the following tasks while you time them: say the letters of the alphabet, do 10 jumping jacks, say his or her name five times, shake the hands of six people in the room, touch all four corners of the room, etc. Add new tasks or repeat tasks as needed. Older children may take turns giving commands to rest of group. (Optional: Children repeat Psalm 119:60 before doing tasks.)

Conclude

We had fun trying to do these things in a hurry. What does Psalm 119:60 say we should hurry to do? Read verse aloud. **Whose commands are we to obey? When we hurry, or hasten, to obey God's commands, it means that we don't try to put off doing what God wants. Because God's commands help us know the best way to live, we are ready and glad to obey them.** Pray, thanking God for His commands and asking His help in following them.

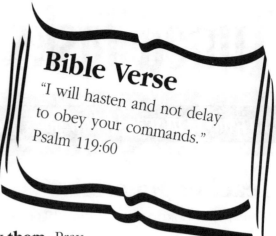

Bible Verse
"I will hasten and not delay to obey your commands."
Psalm 119:60

Discussion Questions

1. **What are some other things you can do quickly?**

2. **What kinds of things do you like to take your time to do?**

3. **Why do you think God wants us to hurry to obey His commands?** (To not waste time. So we don't forget to obey.)

4. **God tells us to treat others honestly and fairly. How can you be ready to quickly obey this command during the week?** (Always tell the truth. Be fair when sharing toys or snacks.)

Emergency Kit

God helps us do what's right, even when it's hard.

Teacher Materials

Large bag with these objects inside: Bible with bookmark at Psalm 119:66, eraser and a framed photo of a friend and/or family member.

Bible Verse

"Teach me knowledge and good judgment, for I believe in your commands." Psalm 119:66

Introduce the Object Talk

A first-aid or emergency kit usually has bandages and medicine in it. This bag is like an emergency kit for people who love God. Let's find out what's in the bag.

Present the Object Talk

1. Show bag to children and shake it slightly, so children hear objects inside. Invite one or more volunteers to feel the outside of the bag and try to guess what the objects might be.

2. As you take each item out of the bag one at a time, explain how the object reminds us of what it means to do what's right.

This eraser reminds us of making mistakes. Obeying God doesn't mean we'll never make mistakes. God erases our wrong actions by forgiving our sins when we ask Him to.

This picture of a friend reminds us that God gives us moms and dads, grandmas and grandpas, sisters and brothers and friends who will pray for us and help us know what God wants us to do.

Conclude

The best part of obeying God is that God gives us the Bible to help us obey Him. Read Psalm 119:66 aloud. **To have good judgment means to be wise and know the right things to do and say. We know that we can depend on God to help us be wise and make good choices.** Ask God's help in doing what's right.

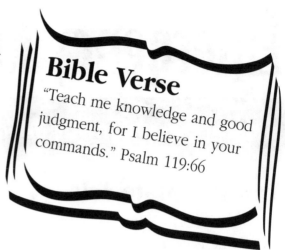

Bible Verse

"Teach me knowledge and good judgment, for I believe in your commands." Psalm 119:66

Discussion Questions

1. **What promises in God's Word do you remember? instructions?** Tell an example of a promise or instruction that has helped you obey God. Older children may find and read a promise or two: Joshua 1:9; Psalm 23:1; Proverbs 3:5,6.

2. **Who is someone God has given you to help you learn what God wants you to do?**

Follow the Light

We can learn the very best way to live from God's Word.

Teacher Materials

Bible with bookmark at Psalm 119:105, flashlight, index card on which you have written Psalm 119:105; optional—laser penlight.

Bible Verse
"Your word is a lamp to my feet and a light for my path."
Psalm 119:105

Introduce the Object Talk

God's Word helps us learn to live in the very best way. Because God's Word is so important, it is sometimes compared to a light. Let's use this flashlight to find out how light helps us.

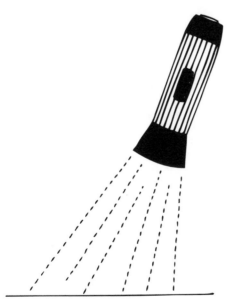

Present the Object Talk

1. While a volunteer covers his or her eyes, hide index card nearby. Volunteer uncovers eyes.

2. Use flashlight to slowly trace on the floor a path which the volunteer follows, eventually leading the volunteer to the location of the hidden card. (Optional: Use laser penlight instead of flashlight.) Volunteer reads verse aloud.

3. Repeat activity with other volunteers as time permits, inviting children to take turns hiding card and using the flashlight. (If you have a large group, use the flashlight to direct volunteer's attention around the room, stopping the light on the location where the card is hidden. Volunteer comes forward to find the card and read it aloud.)

4. Discuss the activity by asking, **How did the flashlight help you? Where did the flashlight lead you?**

Conclude

God's Word, the Bible, is like a light because it shows us the path to follow and the very best way to live. The things we learn in the Bible help us know how to love and obey God. Read Psalm 119:105 aloud. Lead children in prayer, thanking God for His Word.

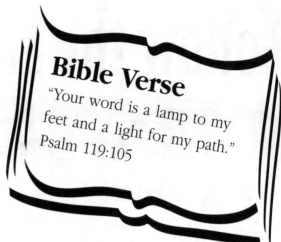

Bible Verse
"Your word is a lamp to my feet and a light for my path."
Psalm 119:105

Discussion Questions

1. When might you need a flashlight or other kind of light to help you find your way?

2. When do kids your age need help to know how to love and obey God? (When someone wants to start an argument. When someone is being unkind.)
How can God's Word help us in those situations? (Helps us know what to say and do. Gives us commands to follow.)

Action Words

God's words are valuable because they show us the best ways to live.

Teacher Materials
Bible with Psalm 119:127 marked with a bookmark.

Introduce the Object Talk
The words we say can't be seen, but they can be powerful. Let's talk about why words—especially God's words—can be so powerful.

Bible Verse
"I love your commands more than gold, more than pure gold." Psalm 119:127

Present the Object Talk

1. Whisper "fire!" to a volunteer who then acts out his or her response to the word. Other children in the group try to identify the word. Give clues as needed to help children guess. After the word is guessed ask, **Why is the word "fire" powerful?** (Gives us important information. Knowing about a fire can save our lives.)

2. Repeat activity with other volunteers and these words or phrases: "stop," "free candy," "home run," "goal," "I'm not it," "dinner's ready," "on your mark—get set—go," "foul ball."

Conclude

Why do you think God's words or commands are so powerful? (They help us know the best way to live. They tell us how to obey God instead of sinning.) **Because God's commands help us in so many ways, the Bible says they are very valuable.** Read Psalm 119:127 aloud. **If this verse were written today, what words might be substituted for the word "gold"?** Pray, thanking God for His commands and asking His help to obey them.

Bible Verse

"I love your commands more than gold, more than pure gold." Psalm 119:127

Discussion Questions

1. **What are some other powerful things that can't be seen?** (Wind. Thunder.)

2. **What are some ways kids your age can show they think God's commands are valuable?**

3. **How has one of God's commands helped you know what to do or say?** Tell children about a time one of God's commands has helped you.

Take It Away

Teacher Materials

Bible with bookmark at Psalm 130:7, clear glass, measuring cup, water, blue food coloring, bleach, spoon; optional—markers, white construction paper.

Bible Verse

"Put your hope in the Lord, for with the Lord is unfailing love and with him is full redemption." Psalm 130:7

Introduce the Object Talk

When we sin, we might feel like God can't love us anymore and that our sin can't be taken away. Watch to see if anything gets taken away in this experiment.

Present the Object Talk

1. Place one cup water in a clear glass. Add three drops of blue food coloring. **How can we take the color out of the water? Can we pour it out?** Volunteers tell ideas.

2. Add a half cup of bleach to glass. Stir and let stand. The water will become clear. NOTE: Keep bleach away from children. (Optional: Draw on white construction paper with markers. Use spoon to add several drops of bleach onto the drawings. Drawings will disappear.)

Conclude

This experiment is an example of a way color can be taken away even when it seems impossible. It reminds me that our sin can be taken away, too. God's love and forgiveness are bigger than our sin. When we ask His forgiveness, He takes away our sin.

Bible Verse
"Put your hope in the Lord, for with the Lord is unfailing love and with him is full redemption." Psalm 130:7

Listen for the last word in this verse: it means something wonderful God does for us. Read Psalm 130:7 aloud. **When something is redeemed, it becomes useful or valuable. This verse reminds us that because God's love for us never ends, we can depend on Him to always treat us as valuable.** Thank God for His unfailing love.

Discussion Questions

1. How does doing wrong often make us feel?

2. Who in your family has forgiven you? How did you feel?

3. When are times kids need to remember God's forgiveness?

4. Why can we depend on God to forgive us? (Because God loves us.)

Full of Beans

God doesn't give up on us.

Teacher Materials

Bible with Psalm 136:1 marked with a book-mark, one bowl or bucket filled with several cups of beans (or dry cereal), one empty bowl or bucket, one teaspoon; optional—additional teaspoons.

Bible Verse
"Give thanks to the Lord, for he is good. His love endures forever." Psalm 136:1

Introduce the Object Talk

God never gives up loving or helping us. As we work together on a big job, see if you feel like giving up.

Present the Object Talk

1. Place the filled bowl or bucket on one side of the room. Place the empty bowl or bucket on the other side of the room. Select six to eight volunteers. Volunteers line up by the filled container. Hand each volunteer a teaspoon.

2. How long do you think it will take to move all these beans to the empty container—one spoonful at a time? Children take turns carrying beans to the empty container. If time is short, give each volunteer a spoon and let them all work at the same time. Several times during the activity ask children how this job makes them feel and make comments such as the following: **Moving all these beans is a big job! A job like this might make you feel like quitting. If we don't give up on this job, it will get done!** Allow the activity to continue until all beans are moved or until children lose interest.

Small Group Option

All children line up and take turns carrying beans to the empty container.

Conclude

One of the things I'm glad to know about God is that He doesn't give up loving us. How does Psalm 136:1 describe God? Read verse aloud. **God is good, and because He is so good He will never give up loving or helping us.** Thank God for His love and help.

Bible Verse

"Give thanks to the Lord, for he is good. His love endures forever." Psalm 136:1

Discussion Questions

1. **What are some jobs you've felt like quitting?**

2. **Why do you think God doesn't quit loving us so much?** (His love is so great!)

3. **How has God shown love and help to you and your family?**

4. **When we've disobeyed God, how do we know God still loves us?** (We can tell God we're sorry for our sin. He cares for us and promises to forgive us.)

Wave Bottles

Jesus is so great that we can't help but praise Him.

Teacher Materials

Bible with bookmark at Psalm 145:3, 12-ounce clear plastic bottle, water, blue food coloring, mineral oil, tape; optional— picture of ocean or starry sky.

Bible Verse
"Great is the Lord and most worthy of praise; his greatness no one can fathom." Psalm 145:3

Prepare the Object Talk

Fill bottle half full with water. Add several drops of blue food coloring. Fill remainder of bottle with mineral oil. Fasten cap tightly and wrap with tape. (If you have a large group, prepare more than one bottle.)

Introduce the Object Talk

The more we get to know about Jesus, the more we want to praise Him. Let's look at something that reminds us of how great Jesus is.

Present the Object Talk

1. Show bottle. Ask a volunteer to hold the bottle horizontally and gently tilt the bottle from end to end, creating a wavelike motion. Allow time for children to experiment with the bottle.

2. The waves in this bottle remind me of the ocean. What words would you use to describe an ocean? How hard do you think it might be to see to the very bottom of the ocean or a deep lake? Why? Volunteers tell ideas. (Optional: Show picture of ocean instead of using wave bottle, or show starry sky picture and talk with children about the impossibility of counting all the stars in the sky.)

Conclude

The ocean is so big and so deep we can't understand exactly what it is like. Listen to what the Bible says about the Lord. Read Psalm 145:3 aloud. **The word "fathom" means to understand. This verse tells us that the Lord is so great we can never understand exactly how great He is! Because Jesus is so great, we want to praise Him.** Lead children in prayer, thanking Jesus for His greatness.

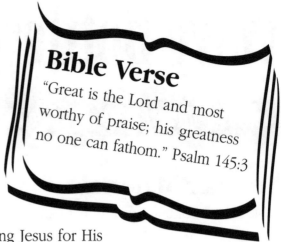

Bible Verse

"Great is the Lord and most worthy of praise; his greatness no one can fathom." Psalm 145:3

Discussion Questions

1. **What are some other things that remind us of how great Jesus is?** (The miracles He did on earth. His resurrection.)

2. **What are some of the ways people praise Jesus for His greatness?** (Sing songs about Him. Pray. Tell others about His greatness.)

3. **What would you like to praise Jesus for?**

Fast and Slow

God is eager to love and forgive us.

Teacher Materials

Bible with bookmark at Psalm 145:8, scratch paper, pencil, coin, crackers; optional—stopwatch or watch with second hand.

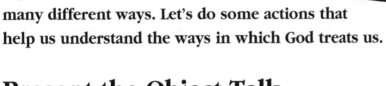

Bible Verse

"The Lord is gracious and compassionate, slow to anger and rich in love." Psalm 145:8

Introduce the Object Talk

God's love and forgiveness are so amazing that the Bible talks about them in many different ways. Let's do some actions that help us understand the ways in which God treats us.

Present the Object Talk

1. Invite volunteers to take turns seeing how slowly and then how quickly they can complete a variety of tasks: do three jumping jacks, write his or her name, crumple up four pieces of paper, flip a coin five times, eat a cracker. Select different volunteers for each fast and slow action. (Optional: Time children using watch, limiting the slow actions to about 30 seconds.) If time is short, ask more than one volunteer to complete tasks at the same time.

2. Your actions were good examples of what it means to do things slowly and what it means to do things quickly. Psalm 145:8 tells us something God is slow to do and something God is quick to do. Read verse aloud. **What does this verse say God is slow to do?** (Be angry.) **What does this verse say God is eager to give us a lot of?** (His love.) **God cares for each of us so much that He is eager and glad to show His love to us. He is quick to forgive us when we've done wrong things.**

Small Group Option

Ask all children to complete the tasks.

Conclude

Lead children in prayer, thanking God for His love and forgiveness.

Bible Verse

"The Lord is gracious and compassionate, slow to anger and rich in love." Psalm 145:8

Discussion Questions

1. **What are some ways in which God has shown His love to us?** (Hears and answers prayer. Gives us courage. Gives what we need every day. Provided a way for us to become members of His family.)

2. **When might kids your age feel as though God doesn't love them?** (When they've done wrong. When they have problems. When prayers aren't answered right away.)

3. **What words can you think of that describe God's love and forgiveness?**

Bigger Than All

God's love and power are bigger than the biggest fear.

Teacher Materials

Bible with Isaiah 12:2 marked with a bookmark, six to eight classroom or household objects ranging in size from very small to very large.

Introduce the Object Talk

When we feel worried or afraid because of problems at school or in our neighborhoods, it helps to remember that God's love and power are bigger than our biggest fears. Let's name some things that are bigger than others.

Present the Object Talk

1. Invite volunteers to arrange objects in order of size. Hand volunteers one object each and have them line up in order.

2. Beginning with the smallest object, invite children to name a variety of objects which are bigger than the smallest object but smaller than the next object. For example, a pencil is bigger than a penny but smaller than a book. Continue until all objects have been discussed. **What are the biggest objects you can think of?** (Redwood tree. Skyscraper. Bridge.)

Conclude

We've been talking about a lot of things that are bigger than others. Listen to Isaiah 12:2 to find out what we can remember about God when we're afraid or worried. Read Isaiah 12:2 aloud. We can remember that God's strength and His help for us are bigger than our fears or worries. Thank God for His love and help when we're worried or afraid.

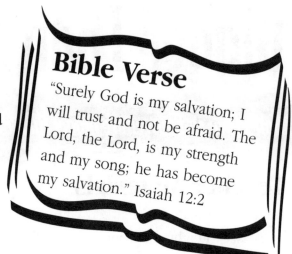

Bible Verse

"Surely God is my salvation; I will trust and not be afraid. The Lord, the Lord, is my strength and my song; he has become my salvation." Isaiah 12:2

Discussion Questions

1. What's a worry a kid your age might have? a fear?

2. Why might someone who's afraid forget about God's love and help?

3. How has God helped you when you've felt afraid?

4. What worry or fear do you want to talk to God about?

Shoe Talk

God chooses all kinds of people to learn from Him.

Teacher Materials

Bible with bookmark at Isaiah 48:17, one shoe from a variety of pairs of shoes (tennis, dress, sandal, slipper, boot, cleats, etc.) in a bag.

Bible Verse

"I am the Lord your God, who teaches you what is best for you, who directs you in the way you should go." Isaiah 48:17

Introduce the Object Talk

Even though God has made each person different, He wants each of us to learn about Him. Look at the things in this bag that remind us of the different ways in which God has made us and what He wants us to do.

Present the Object Talk

1. Invite volunteers to take turns removing shoes, one at a time, from the bag. As each shoe is shown ask, **What kind of shoe is this? How is it different from other kinds of shoes? How is it the same? When might someone wear this shoe? What makes this shoe useful?**

2. When all the shoes have been shown and discussed say, **Even though these are all shoes, they are all different from each other. In the same way, we're all people made by God, but we are different from each other, too. All these different kinds of shoes remind me that God has chosen many different kinds of people to learn from Him.**

Conclude

These shoes also remind me of walking down a path or a street. **Listen to Isaiah 48:17 to find out who will help us know the right ways to act.** Read Isaiah 48:17 aloud. **Who does this verse say will teach us and help us learn the best way to live?** Lead children in prayer, thanking God for inviting each of us to learn from Him and for teaching us about Him.

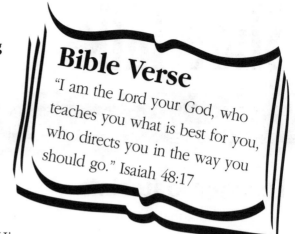

Bible Verse

"I am the Lord your God, who teaches you what is best for you, who directs you in the way you should go." Isaiah 48:17

Discussion Questions

1. **What are some other kinds of shoes you wear? How are they alike or different?**

2. **How did God make people alike? How did He make them different?**

3. **What are some of the ways people today can learn more about God?** (Hear Bible stories. Talk to others who love and obey God.)

4. **What can you do this week to learn about God?**

What's Dependable?

No matter how bad things look, depend on God because He is in control.

Teacher Materials

Bible with bookmark at Jeremiah 17:7, a variety of familiar objects (alarm clock, ruler, pen, flashlight, dictionary, measuring cup, TV remote, etc.).

Bible Verse

"Blessed is the man who trusts in the Lord, whose confidence is in him." Jeremiah 17:7

Introduce the Object Talk

We all need help when we have problems, feel worried or don't know what to do. God's Word tells us that in any situation we can be confident that God will help us. Let's find out why we can depend on God more than any object or person.

Present the Object Talk

Show each object one at a time. Invite volunteers to answer these questions about each object: **What is this object used for? When have you used this object? How did this object help you? Why can you depend on this item to help you? When can't you depend on this item to help you?**

Conclude

Even though these items can help us and give us true information in many situations, sometimes they can't help us. Listen to this Bible verse to find out whom we can depend on in ANY situation, no matter how bad things look. Read Jeremiah 17:7 aloud. **Why can we be confident in God's help?** (He is more powerful than anything in the world. He loves us and promises to be with us.) Lead children in prayer, thanking God for His help and that He is always with us.

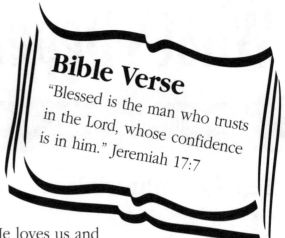

Bible Verse

"Blessed is the man who trusts in the Lord, whose confidence is in him." Jeremiah 17:7

Discussion Questions

1. **What are some other objects that you depend on?** (Car. Bike. Computer.) **Why might these items not always be dependable?** (Cars break down. Bikes get flat tires. Computers "crash.")

2. **What are some times when kids your age need to depend on God's help? people older than you? younger than you?**

3. **What can you do when you need to remember God's help?** (Pray to Him. Remember a Bible verse about His power and help.)

Animal Talk

God is big enough to care for us in all situations.

Teacher Materials

Bible with a bookmark at Nahum 1:7, large sheet of paper, marker; optional—pictures of the animals discussed below.

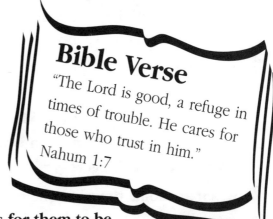

Bible Verse

"The Lord is good, a refuge in times of trouble. He cares for those who trust in him." Nahum 1:7

Introduce the Object Talk

A refuge is a place of safety. Because God is so great, He is like a refuge for us. He also cares for His creation by making ways for them to be safe. Let's discover some ways in which God made refuges for animals.

Present the Object Talk

1. On large sheet of paper, draw nine blank lines, one for each letter of the word "porcupine." Volunteers guess letters of the alphabet. As each correct letter is guessed, write it on the appropriate blank line. When an incorrect letter is guessed, write it to the side of the blank lines. Volunteers keep guessing letters until the word is identified. **What did God give a porcupine to help keep it safe?** (Quills that stand up when a porcupine is afraid.)

2. Repeat game with other animals: chameleon—able to change skin color, so it is less noticeable; gorilla—usually peaceful and shy but beats chest and screams when afraid; ostrich—largest bird in the world and can protect itself with a very powerful kick; snowshoe hare—grows white coat in winter to help it hide from attackers; alpine marmot—hides in rocks and whistles to other marmots when danger is present; mountain goat—special pads on hoofs stop it from slipping on steep rocks; sea otter—two layers of fur give warmth in cold ocean water.

_ _ _ r _ u _ _ _ E

z T s A

Conclude

God made these animals in special ways to help them stay safe when they are in danger. **God is like a refuge for us, too.** Read Nahum 1:7 aloud. **What does God do for the people who believe and trust in Him?** (Promises to answer prayers. Gives courage.) Thank God for His loving care and for helping us when we are in danger or feel afraid.

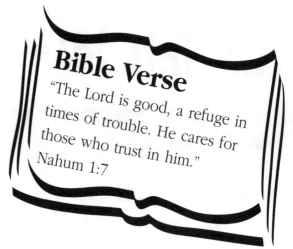

Bible Verse

"The Lord is good, a refuge in times of trouble. He cares for those who trust in him." Nahum 1:7

Discussion Questions

1. What are some other ways in which God made animals so that they are protected from danger?

2. When are some times people need God's help to keep them safe?

3. Who are some people God has given you to help you stay safe?

4. What are some other ways God shows His care for you?

It's Free!

When we love God, we give generously.

Teacher Materials

Bible with bookmark at Matthew 10:8, marker, one index card per child and one bite-sized snack item, sticker or small prize for each child.

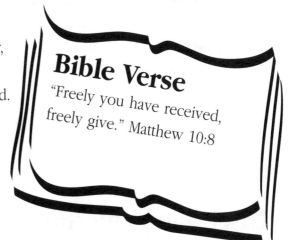

Bible Verse

"Freely you have received, freely give." Matthew 10:8

Prepare the Object Talk

Print the word "FREE" on several cards. Shuffle "FREE" cards in with blank cards.

Introduce the Object Talk

Everyone likes to get something for free! The Bible tells us that even though His love is more valuable than anything in the world, Jesus freely gives it to us. Today we're going to get something for free and talk about how we can give freely to God and to others.

Present the Object Talk

1. Give each child a card, keeping cards facedown.

2. At your signal, children pass cards facedown around the group. When you signal "stop," each child looks at his or her card. Children holding cards marked "FREE" get (snacks) for themselves and pass out (snacks) to other children.

Small Group Option

1. Print only one "FREE" card. Shuffle "FREE" card in with blank cards. Seat children in a circle. At your signal, children pass cards facedown around the circle.

2. When you signal "stop," child holding "FREE" card gets a (snack) for him- or herself and gives a (snack) to one other child. Repeat the activity until all children have received a (snack).

Bible Verse

"Freely you have received, freely give." Matthew 10:8

Conclude

In this activity we received our (snacks) for free. Matthew 10:8 talks about the way in which Jesus gives us what we need. Read verse aloud. **Jesus said these words when He was telling His followers to help and care for others. Jesus has given His love to us for free! We don't have to do anything to earn it!** Lead children in prayer, thanking God for His free gift of love and asking His help in giving freely in return.

Discussion Questions

1. What are some other things God freely gives us? (Answers to prayer. Forgiveness of sins. Friends and family.)

2. What can we give to God that money can't buy? (Our love. Our obedience.)

3. What can we give to others that money can't buy? (Friendship. Honesty. Patience. The good news about Jesus.)

Choose That Gift!

Teacher Materials

Bible with bookmark at Matthew 22:37, one large box, one small box, penny, dollar bill, heavy nonbreakable item (book, brick, etc.), wrapping paper, scissors, tape, ribbon.

Bible Verse

"Love the Lord your God with all your heart and with all your soul and with all your mind." Matthew 22:37

Prepare the Object Talk

Place the penny and nonbreakable item in the large box and wrap it. Place the dollar in the small box and wrap it.

Introduce the Object Talk

Loving God is something we can show not only with our actions but also in our attitudes—the way we think about things. Sometimes a person might say and do one thing but think something totally different. See if you can figure out what's really on the inside of these gifts.

Present the Object Talk

1. Place wrapped boxes on table or floor, so children can see them.

2. Invite several volunteers to take turns examining and shaking boxes.

3. Ask children to raise hands showing which of the two boxes they would like to receive. Ask several volunteers to tell why they chose the boxes and what they think is inside.

4. Have two volunteers open boxes and show the contents.

Conclude

What made some people think the biggest box was best? What made some people think the smallest box was best? Sometimes the way people or things look on the outside isn't the same as how they are on the inside. Listen to what Matthew 22:37 says about what should be on the inside—or in the attitudes—of God's followers. Read verse aloud. **When we love God with our attitudes, we want to please Him in everything we do. Loving and obeying God is what's most important to us.** Pray, expressing your love for God and thanking Him for His love for all people.

Bible Verse

"Love the Lord your God with all your heart and with all your soul and with all your mind." Matthew 22:37

Discussion Questions

1. When have you been given a gift that was better than it looked on the outside? eaten a food that tasted better than it looked?

2. How do people show love for their friends and family members?

3. What are some ways in which people show their love for God?

4. How has God shown He loves you? How can you show your love for Him?

Balloon Pop

Because Jesus is alive, we know He will keep His promise to be with us now and forever.

Teacher Materials

Bible with bookmark at Matthew 28:20, two large balloons, transparent tape, sewing needle; optional—additional balloons.

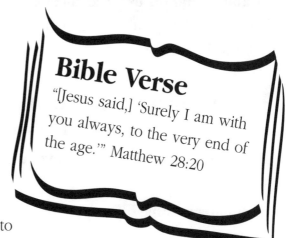

Bible Verse

"[Jesus said,] 'Surely I am with you always, to the very end of the age.'" Matthew 28:20

Prepare the Object Talk

Inflate (a little less than full) and tie the balloons. Place a 2-inch (5-cm) strip of tape at end of one balloon. Smooth over the tape to remove all air bubbles. Before class, practice Step 2 below.

Introduce the Object Talk

All through our lives we need help—especially when things happen that make us afraid. Because Jesus is alive, He can protect and help us. Look at these balloons to find out what protects them.

Present the Object Talk

1. Hold up the needle and the balloon without the tape. **What will happen when I poke the balloon with the needle? The balloon doesn't have any protection against the sharp needle, so it will pop.** Use the needle to pop the balloon.

2. Hold up the second balloon. Firmly push the needle through the tape, keeping a good grasp on the needle. Then smoothly remove the needle. **Why didn't this balloon pop?** Volunteers tell ideas. **This balloon didn't pop when I poked it with the needle because it had something helping it to stay strong and not pop.**

Show children the tape on the balloon. (Optional: Depending on the number of children in your group and their ages, invite children to blow up balloons and attempt to pop them with and without tape.)

Conclude

Jesus promises to help us. Because Jesus is alive, we know He will keep His promises to us. Listen to Jesus' promise. Read Matthew 28:20 aloud. **Jesus promises to be with us now and forever, helping us and caring for us.** Lead children in prayer, thanking Jesus for His promise to be with us.

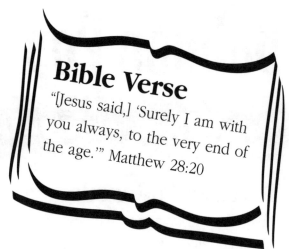

Bible Verse
"[Jesus said,] 'Surely I am with you always, to the very end of the age.'" Matthew 28:20

Discussion Questions

1. When do people need to know of Jesus' help?

2. When are some times kids your age need to remember that Jesus is with them?

3. What are some other promises Jesus makes to His followers? (To hear and answer their prayers. To forgive sins.)

Worldwide Singing

We can celebrate with people all over the world the birth of God's Son, sent by God to keep His promise of a Savior.

Teacher Materials

Bible with bookmark at Luke 2:11, world map or globe; optional—a player and recording of "Silent Night" in a foreign language.

Bible Verse

"Today in the town of David a Savior has been born to you; he is Christ the Lord." Luke 2:11

Introduce the Object Talk

The angels' message about Jesus' birth was such good news that people all over the world celebrate Jesus' birthday. Let's look at some of the places where people believe in Jesus and sing songs about His birth.

Present the Object Talk

1. Show map or globe and point out the area where your church is located. (Optional: Older children may find locations.)

2. Read Luke 2:11. **Another name for the town of David is Bethlehem.** Locate Bethlehem on map or globe. **In the Old Testament part of the Bible, prophets told about God's promise to send His Son to be born in Bethlehem.**

3. **What are the names of some Christmas carols you remember?** Volunteers tell answers. **"Silent Night" is one of the most famous Christmas carols. This carol was first written in Germany.** Locate Germany on map or globe. **A pastor of a church wrote a poem about Jesus' birth in Bethlehem. He gave the poem as a Christmas gift to his friend Franz Gruber. Later that same night, Mr. Gruber wrote a melody to go with the words. Everyone who heard the carol liked the words so much that the carol spread all over the world.** (Optional: Sing "Silent Night" with children, play recording of the carol in a foreign language or ask someone to sing the carol in another language.)

Conclude

When we sing carols like "Silent Night," we can think about the thousands and thousands of people all over the world who sing this song in their own languages. Let's thank God for sending His Son to be born. Lead children in prayer.

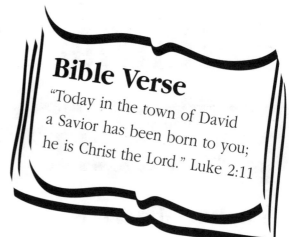

Bible Verse
"Today in the town of David a Savior has been born to you; he is Christ the Lord." Luke 2:11

Discussion Questions

1. What are some of the ways that people in our country celebrate Jesus' birth?

2. What are the ways that people in other countries remember Jesus' birth?
(People in Mexico act out the story of Joseph and Mary looking for a place to stay. Christians in Israel plant seeds in front of nativity scenes; the growing seeds remind people of new life.)

3. What is your favorite song to sing about Jesus' birth?

Here's Jesus!

Jesus' baptism and John's announcement help everyone know that Jesus is the Savior.

Teacher Materials

Bible with bookmark at John 1:29, a variety of newspaper and/or magazine ads and announcements (classified ad, product advertisement, notice of sale at a store, announcement of a coming event, etc.).

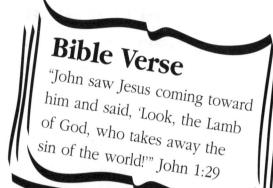

Bible Verse
"John saw Jesus coming toward him and said, 'Look, the Lamb of God, who takes away the sin of the world!'" John 1:29

Introduce the Object Talk

In the Bible, the good news about Jesus was announced by John the Baptist. Today we hear about good news in lots of different ways. Look at these announcements to find what news is being told.

Present the Object Talk

1. One at a time show the ads and announcements you collected. Ask a volunteer to describe the message of each ad or announcement. **What are some other ways in which announcements are made?** (Birth or graduation announcements. Billboards. TV or radio commercials.)

2. All of these announcements tell things that will soon happen. But after a few weeks—after the sale is over or after the event has happened—we don't

really need to remember the announcement any more. The announcement John made about Jesus, however, is something people have needed to know about and will remember for a long time! The words John said about Jesus are so important that EVERYONE still needs to hear them. Read John 1:29 aloud.

Conclude

What kind of ad or billboard would you make to announce this good news about Jesus? Volunteers tell ideas. Lead children in prayer, thanking God for the good news that Jesus is His Son.

Bible Verse

"John saw Jesus coming toward him and said, 'Look, the Lamb of God, who takes away the sin of the world!'" John 1:29

Discussion Questions

1. **Why was Jesus called the "Lamb of God"?**

   ("Lamb of God" is a name for Jesus that tells us that He died to take away our sins. Jewish people used to offer a lamb as a sacrifice to God for their sins; Jesus became like one of those lambs when He died.)

2. **What other news about Jesus would you like to announce to others?**

3. **How would you announce the good news about Jesus?**

Rainbow Fun

Teacher Materials

Bible with bookmark at John 14:15; six glasses; measuring cup; light corn syrup; glycerin (found in most pharmacies); water; cooking oil; rubbing alcohol; red, yellow, green and blue food coloring; four spoons.

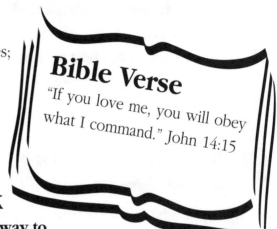

Bible Verse
"If you love me, you will obey what I command." John 14:15

Introduce the Object Talk

God's instructions help us know the best way to live. Watch what happens when I follow these instructions.

Present the Object Talk

Read directions aloud as you complete each step. Or have an older child read aloud as you work.

1. Set out the glasses and pour a half cup of each liquid into separate glasses in the following order: light corn syrup, glycerin, water, cooking oil, rubbing alcohol.

2. Using separate spoons, stir several drops of food coloring into the liquids: red into light corn syrup, yellow into glycerin, green into water, none into cooking oil, blue into alcohol.

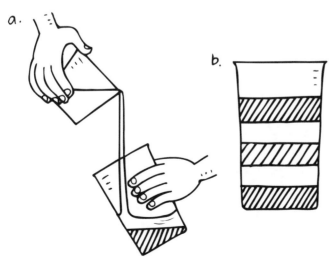

3. Pour about 1 inch (2.5 cm) of each liquid into the remaining glass as follows: *(a)* pour red into the center of the glass without letting liquid hit the side; *(b)* tilt the glass and pour yellow into point where red meets the side of the glass (see sketch a); *(c)* pour green liquid down the side of the tilted glass; then clear; then blue.

Each liquid should float on the top of the previous liquid. Hold the glass upright to see rainbow (see sketch b).

Bible Verse
"If you love me, you will obey what I command." John 14:15

Conclude

Following these directions helped me make a rainbow. Following God's directions, or commands, is even better! They help us know the best way to live. Read John 14:15 aloud. **Because I love God, I want to obey Him.** Ask God's help in obeying.

Discussion Questions

1. What would have happened if I hadn't followed the directions?

2. Being honest is a direction, or command, God wants us to obey. What are some of the results of being honest? (Parents and friends trust you and like to be with you. Teachers know they can depend on you.)

3. What are some ways you can show love for God and obey His commands? (Be honest. Care about the needs of others.)

Measure Up!

Teacher Materials

Bible with bookmark at John 15:13, a variety of items used for measuring—ruler, measuring stick, thermometer, rain gauge, measuring cup, tape measure, scale.

Bible Verse
"Greater love has no one than this, that he lay down his life for his friends." John 15:13

Introduce the Object Talk

When we want to find out how big something is, we measure it. But there's one thing that is so great it can't be measured. As we measure some things today, be thinking about what this great thing might be.

Present the Object Talk

One at a time, show each measuring item. Allow children time to experiment with each item. If possible, children measure themselves and/or other items in room.

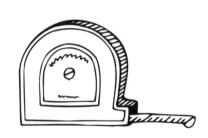

Discuss items used for measuring: **What does this item measure? What's something small this item might measure? What might be the biggest thing this item could measure?**

Conclude

It's fun to measure all kinds of different items. Listen to what the Bible says is so great. Read John 15:13 aloud. **Who is this verse talking about?** (Jesus.) **What does this verse say Jesus did? Why did Jesus give up His life?** (To show His love for us.) **Jesus loves us so much He was willing to die, taking the punishment for our sins. His love for us can't be measured.**
Lead children in prayer, thanking Jesus for His great love.

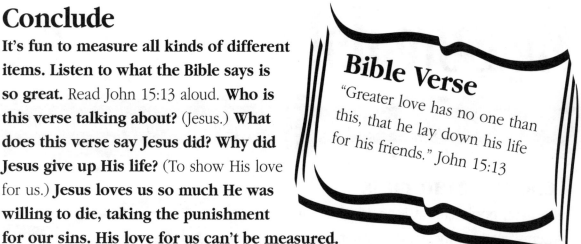

Bible Verse
"Greater love has no one than this, that he lay down his life for his friends." John 15:13

Discussion Questions

1. **What are some other words you would use to describe Jesus' love? Why can't Jesus' love be measured?** (It's too big!)

2. **How does Jesus show His love for us today?** (Forgives our sins. Promises always to be with us and help us. Hears and answers our prayers.)

3. **When Jesus lived on earth, what else did He do to show His great love?** (Taught people about God. Healed sick people. Cared for many people.)

You've Got Mail!

The Bible is God's true story and reading it helps us know and love Him.

Teacher Materials

Bag into which you have placed a Bible with bookmark at John 20:31 and a variety of mail (bill, letter, greeting card, advertisement, catalog, e-mail, magazine, etc.).

Bible Verse
"These are written that you may believe that Jesus is the Christ, the Son of God, and that by believing you may have life in his name." John 20:31

Introduce the Object Talk

The Bible is like a letter from God—written just to me and you. In this bag I've got a sample of some of the mail I received this week. As I take the mail out of the bag, let's talk about how God's letter is different from the rest of the mail.

Present the Object Talk

1. One at a time, hold up each piece of mail (keeping the Bible until the last) and ask volunteers to describe it. Discuss mail by asking questions such as, **Who is this mail from? What is this mail trying to get me to do? What message does this mail tell me? Why might I be excited to get this mail?**

2. Hold up the Bible. **How would you describe this letter? How is God's letter to us different from the rest of the mail I've received?** (It was written long ago. Its message is for everyone.) **What makes God's Word better than any other message to us?** (It's true. It tells the good news about Jesus.)

Conclude

Read John 20:31 aloud. **The words in the Bible help each person learn that when we believe Jesus is God's Son, we can be part of God's family.** Talk with interested children about becoming Christians. (Follow guidelines in "Leading a Child to Christ," p. 12.) Thank God for sending His letter to each of us and ask His help in getting to know more about Him as we read the Bible.

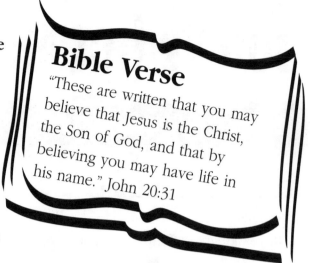

Bible Verse

"These are written that you may believe that Jesus is the Christ, the Son of God, and that by believing you may have life in his name." John 20:31

Discussion Questions

1. What's your favorite kind of mail?

2. What's the best thing you've ever received in the mail?

3. When are some times you read God's letter—the Bible?

Overflowing Love

God's gift of the Holy Spirit made it possible for the family of believers to grow as they showed God's love and care.

Teacher Materials

Bible with bookmark at Romans 5:5, small or medium-sized glass jar, large baking pan with sides, measuring utensils, baking soda, vinegar, food coloring.

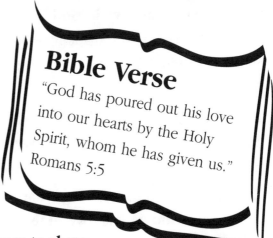

Bible Verse

"God has poured out his love into our hearts by the Holy Spirit, whom he has given us." Romans 5:5

Introduce the Object Talk

The Holy Spirit is God at work in our lives or in the world. God's gift of the Holy Spirit makes it possible for His followers to show love and care for others. When we accept God's love, it overflows to others. Watch to see what overflows in this experiment.

Present the Object Talk

1. Set the jar in the middle of the baking pan. Pour one tablespoon of baking soda into the jar. Measure one cup of vinegar and add several drops of food coloring to the cup. Pour vinegar into the jar. The liquid will bubble up and overflow the jar.

2. When the vinegar and baking soda were mixed together, they formed a gas called carbon dioxide. The gas pushed the liquid out the top of the jar so that the liquid overflowed.

Conclude

The Bible talks about how God's love can overflow. Read Romans 5:5 aloud. **God loves us so much He wants each of us to show His love to others. God showed His love to us by sending the Holy Spirit. The Holy Spirit helps us show love to others so that the family of people who believe in God can grow.** Lead children in prayer, thanking God for sending the Holy Spirit and asking His help in showing His love to others.

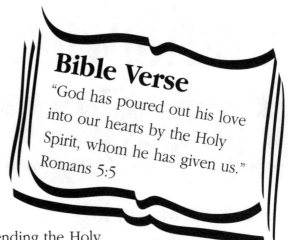

Bible Verse

"God has poured out his love into our hearts by the Holy Spirit, whom he has given us." Romans 5:5

Discussion Questions

1. **What are some other things you have seen that overflow?** (A river or lake that overflows its banks. A soda can that has been shaken before opening.)

2. **God made all these things that overflow. What are some of the other ways God has shown His love to us?**

3. **What are some ways we can show God's love to others?**

4. **How has someone shown God's love to you?**

Dead or Alive?

Jesus' death and resurrection were the fulfillment of God's promise of salvation.

Teacher Materials

Bible with bookmark at Romans 6:4, two each of several examples of fruits with pits (avocados, peaches, olives, dates, plums), knife.

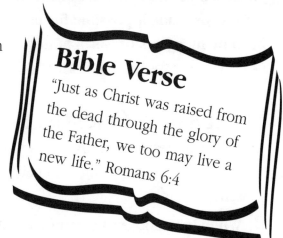

Bible Verse

"Just as Christ was raised from the dead through the glory of the Father, we too may live a new life." Romans 6:4

Prepare the Object Talk

Before children arrive, cut open one of each kind of fruit and remove the pit.

Introduce the Object Talk

All through the Old Testament, we read about God's promise to send a Savior. God kept His promise through Jesus' death and resurrection. Let's look at these reminders of how something that looks dead can grow new life.

Present the Object Talk

1. One at a time, show each fruit pit. **What fruit do you think this pit is from? Does the pit look dead or alive? Why? What would happen if this pit were planted in good soil and watered?**

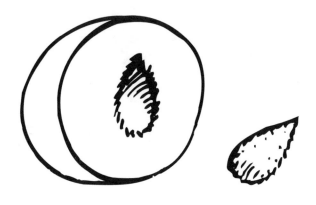

2. Show each fruit. Invite children to match fruit with their pits. After each fruit and pit are matched correctly, comment, **Even though the pits, or seeds, look like they are dead, new plants are able to grow from them.**

Conclude

When Jesus died, His friends thought they would never see Him again. But God's power made Jesus come back to life again. Read Romans 6:4 aloud. What does this verse say we may have because of Jesus' death and resurrection? (A new life.) Jesus made it possible for us to become members of God's family. Thank God in prayer for His gift of salvation.

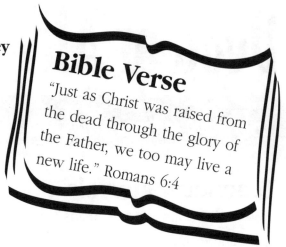

Bible Verse

"Just as Christ was raised from the dead through the glory of the Father, we too may live a new life." Romans 6:4

Discussion Questions

1. **Why was Jesus the only One who could take the punishment for our sins?** (Jesus is the only person who never sinned. He is the One God promised to send.)

2. **When we choose to become members of God's family, what does He give us?** (Forgiveness for our sins. Eternal life.)

3. **What are some other things in nature that remind us of new life?** (Flowers. Baby animals. Butterflies.)

Paid in Full

Becoming a Christian is more than knowing facts about God. God invites each of us to choose to belong to God's family and accept Jesus' love.

Teacher Materials

Bible with bookmark at Romans 6:23, large sheet of paper, marker, calculator, blank check, pen.

Bible Verse

"The wages of sin is death, but the gift of God is eternal life in Christ Jesus our Lord." Romans 6:23

Introduce the Object Talk

God wants us to be part of His family so much that He made it possible for us to receive His love and forgiveness for the wrong things we do. Let's find out how Jesus paid for our sins.

Present the Object Talk

1. If we were to owe money for the wrong actions we've done, we would probably owe a lot of money. Ask children to name wrong actions. (Lying, stealing, cheating, fighting, etc.) As you list each wrong action on paper, have class decide on a dollar amount as penalty, or punishment, for each action (for example, $100 for lying), and write this amount next to the action. Ask a volunteer to add the amounts on the calculator and announce total to class. (Optional: Depending on the age of your group, you may add amounts on the calculator yourself.)

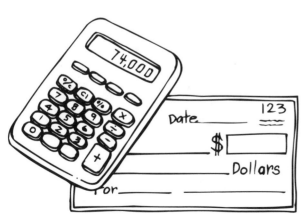

2. If someone loved you enough, he or she could pay what you owe for your wrong actions by writing a check for the full amount. Write out a check for the total amount, leaving the "to" and "from" portions blank.

Conclude

The good news we read in the Bible is that the amount or punishment owed for our sin has been completely paid by Jesus, God's Son. Read Romans 6:23 aloud. **When Jesus died on the cross, He made it possible for our sin to be paid in full so that we can be part of God's family. What a great gift He gave us!** Complete the check, making the check out to "God," signing it from "Jesus" and writing "For (your name)'s sin" in the check memo portion. Lead children in prayer, thanking God for His gift of salvation.

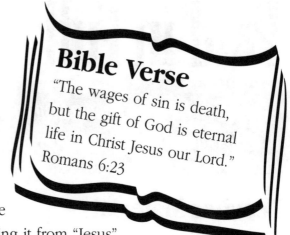

Bible Verse

"The wages of sin is death, but the gift of God is eternal life in Christ Jesus our Lord."
Romans 6:23

Discussion Questions

1. How does doing wrong usually make a person feel?

2. How can asking God to forgive our sins help us? (God promises to give us forgiveness and make us members of His family.)

3. How do we know that God's love is big enough to forgive all the wrong things we and others do? (The Bible tells us so. God always keeps His promises.)

4. How have you learned about God's love for you? (From reading God's Word. From people who show God's love to others.)

Circle Talk

Used 1-11-04

God's love is for everyone, not just people like us.

Teacher Materials

Bible with bookmark at Romans 15:7, large sheet of paper, marker.

Prepare the Object Talk

Draw two large intersecting circles (called a Venn diagram) on a large sheet of paper (see sketch).

Bible Verse

"Accept one another, then, just as Christ accepted you, in order to bring praise to God." Romans 15:7

Introduce the Object Talk

It's important to remember that God's love is for everyone. Let's find out what some of the people whom God loves are like.

Present the Object Talk

Write the names of two volunteers at the top of each circle. Then interview them to find several differences and similarities between them, writing the similarities in the overlapping area of the circles and writing the differences in the remaining areas of the circles. **What do you like to do at school? What is your favorite TV show? favorite color? favorite food? What color are your eyes?** As you fill out the diagram, talk about the ways children are the same and different. **God made people alike in some ways and different in others.** Continue activity with other volunteers and new circles.

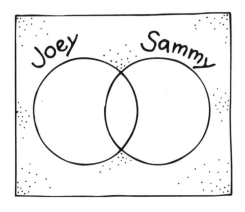

Small Group Option

Group children into pairs. Give each pair a Venn diagram and invite them to draw pictures or write words to show their differences and similarities.

Bible Verse

"Accept one another, then, just as Christ accepted you, in order to bring praise to God." Romans 15:7

Conclude

Listen to Romans 15:7 to find out what God wants us to do for each other whether we are alike or different. Read verse aloud. **When we accept others, it means that we want to show God's love by telling them the good news about Jesus and treating them in kind and fair ways. God's love is for everyone.** Write "Loved by God" in overlapping area of circles. Pray, thanking God for His love and asking His help in showing love to others.

Discussion Questions

1. **How are you alike or different from the people in your family? a friend in your neighborhood or class at school?**

2. **How do you think you might be alike or different from a kid your age who lives in a country far away from here?**

3. **How might you help someone who is different from you learn about God's love? How might you accept that person and treat him or her fairly?** (Invite him or her to go to church or the park. Speak up when others are picking on him or her.)

Zigzag Pictures

No matter where you are or what happens in your life, you can experience God's goodness and live as God wants you to.

Teacher Materials

Bible with bookmark at 1 Corinthians 2:9, two identically sized magazine pictures, sheet of paper that is the same height and twice as wide as one picture, ruler, scissors, glue.

Bible Verse
"No eye has seen, no ear has heard, no mind has conceived what God has prepared for those who love him." 1 Corinthians 2:9

Prepare the Object Talk

Accordion-fold the paper and both pictures, making each pleat about 1 inch (2.5 cm) wide. Open up the pictures and cut along the folded lines. (Discard any end pieces less than 1 inch [2.5 cm] wide.) Glue alternating strips of the pictures in order to the sheet of paper. Fold up the paper.

Introduce the Object Talk

We can't see ahead to what will happen to us; but we know that no matter where we are or what happens to us, God is with us, giving us the good things we need. All through the Bible, God's people discovered how good it is to follow God. Look at this paper to discover two pictures.

Present the Object Talk

1. Show the paper to children, holding it at an angle so that only one picture can be seen. Ask volunteers to describe what they see. Then show paper from another angle to show the other picture.

2. Allow time for children to experiment with holding the paper to see both zigzag pictures.

Conclude

When we looked at the paper, we discovered two pictures. The Bible tells us about something we haven't seen yet, but we'll discover as we grow older. Read 1 Corinthians 2:9 aloud. **This verse helps us remember that we can experience God's love and goodness now and in the future.** Lead children in prayer, thanking Him for His love and for the good things He gives us.

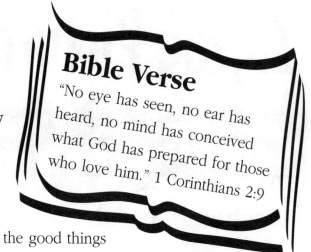

Bible Verse

"No eye has seen, no ear has heard, no mind has conceived what God has prepared for those who love him." 1 Corinthians 2:9

Discussion Questions

1. **What are some of the good things God gives the people who love and obey Him?** (Courage. Wisdom to make good choices. Answers to prayer.)

2. **How has God helped you and your family in the past? What good things has He provided for you?**

3. **How has God helped our church?**

4. **What can you do to show your love for God?**

Who Am I?

Used 1/25/04

Jesus teaches us to live in ways that show we belong to Him and follow Him.

Teacher Materials

Bible with bookmark at Ephesians 4:1, a variety of objects that represent occupations or hobbies (computer disk, gardening glove, book, wrench, basketball, paintbrush, guitar); optional—blindfold.

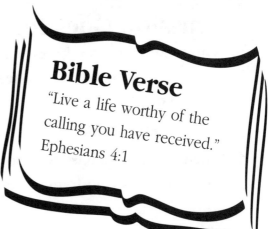

Bible Verse
"Live a life worthy of the calling you have received."
Ephesians 4:1

Introduce the Object Talk

Our friends and families can learn from our words and actions whether or not we have chosen to belong to Jesus and follow Him. The things we do and say every day help people learn about us. See if you can learn what people are like by looking at objects they might use.

Present the Object Talk

1. Show one of the objects you collected. (Optional: Blindfold a volunteer who feels the object and then identifies it.) Children tell what they learn about a person who uses the object. For example, if the object is a gardening glove, children might say "likes to be outdoors," "grows lots of plants" and "works hard."

2. We can tell what a person is like by the things they do and say. Jesus talks about the words and actions of people whose job it is to follow Him— people who are called Christians. What might Christians do to show that they belong to Jesus? (Be honest. Help others. Forgive others. Depend on God to give them what is needed. Say kind words to enemies. Don't put bad things into their bodies.) **Christians do these good things to show their love for God.**

Conclude

Reading the Bible helps us learn ways of showing we belong to Jesus. And we learn that God promises to help us obey Him. Read Ephesians 4:1 aloud. Pray, asking God's help in following Him.

Bible Verse

"Live a life worthy of the calling you have received."
Ephesians 4:1

Discussion Questions

1. **Who is someone you know whose actions show they belong to Jesus? What does that person say and do?**

2. **When is a time a kid your age can show they follow Jesus? How?**

3. **When might it be hard to follow Jesus? What can we do when we need help loving and obeying Jesus?**

Balloon Drop

Loving God means loving all kinds of people.

Teacher Materials

Bible with bookmark at Ephesians 4:2, balloons; optional—balls.

Introduce the Object Talk

The Bible is full of stories about what it means to love God. One way to love God is to show His love to all kinds of people by caring about their needs. Let's watch someone in our group try to help another person.

Present the Object Talk

1. Invite a volunteer to stand next to you. **Let's see how many balloons (Kaitlyn) can hold.** Ask other volunteers to blow up balloons and give them to volunteer to hold. (Optional: To save time, blow up balloons beforehand or use balls instead of balloons.)

2. When volunteer cannot hold any more balloons, ask him or her to help you with a task (open or shut a door, find verse in Bible, etc.). After volunteer expresses difficulty in helping you while still holding onto the balloons, ask, **What would you have to do in order to help me?** (Drop the balloons.) **When others need our help, sometimes we need to drop what we're doing or put aside until later something we're doing so that we can help them.**

Conclude

Listen to Ephesians 4:2 to find the word that describes someone who thinks about what others need instead of always thinking about him- or herself. Read Ephesians 4:2 aloud. **Someone who is humble cares about other people and wants to help them. What else does this verse say we should do?** (Be patient with others as a way of showing love.) **Ephesians 4:2 doesn't say to care only about people we like or who like us. When we say we love God, it means we want to show His love to all kinds of people.** Lead children in prayer, asking God's help in showing love for Him by caring for others.

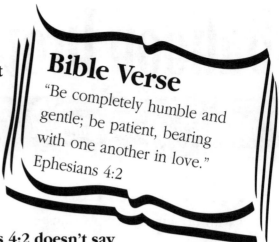

Bible Verse

"Be completely humble and gentle; be patient, bearing with one another in love." Ephesians 4:2

Discussion Questions

1. **In what way has someone been patient with you? helped you with something you needed?**

2. **When might you need to stop doing something in order to help someone who needs help?** (Stop watching TV when parent needs help setting the table. Stop playing a game at recess when a friend gets hurt.)

3. **When might it be hard to do what Jesus wants you to do? What can we do when we need help loving and obeying Jesus?**

Circle Attraction

Giving to others doesn't depend on our wealth because Jesus helps us give more than money.

Teacher Materials

Bible with bookmark at Ephesians 5:2, hole punch, tissue paper, small round balloon.

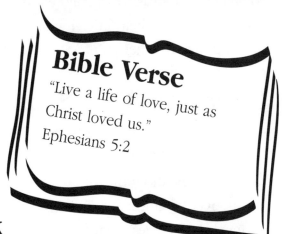

Bible Verse

"Live a life of love, just as Christ loved us."
Ephesians 5:2

Prepare the Object Talk

Use the hole punch to make 20 to 30 tissue-paper circles. Inflate and tie the balloon.

Introduce the Object Talk

Jesus helps us give more than money to others. Our gifts of love can make a big difference. Watch the different actions that take place in this experiment.

Present the Object Talk

1. Place the tissue-paper circles on a table.

2. Rub the balloon against your hair (or a carpet) at least 10 times. Then hold the rubbed side of the balloon several inches (cm) above the paper circles. The paper circles will be attracted to the balloon and jump off the table onto the balloon.

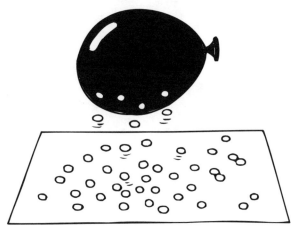

3. As time permits, invite volunteers to take turns creating the attraction between the balloon and the paper circles. (Optional: Provide additional balloons and circles so that more volunteers can participate at once.) **Rubbing the balloon makes an electric charge that attracts, or pulls, the paper circles.**

Conclude

When we show Jesus' love to others, it attracts them to Jesus and helps them want to learn about Jesus. Read Ephesians 5:2. **How does this verse describe the way Jesus' followers should live? What should we be like?** Volunteers tell ideas. Lead children in prayer, asking His help in giving and showing love to others.

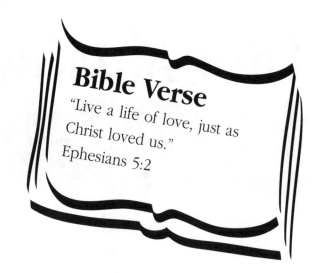

Bible Verse
"Live a life of love, just as Christ loved us."
Ephesians 5:2

Discussion Questions

1. **What other kinds of things attract each other?** (Magnets attract many metal items. Flowers attract bees. Gravity attracts, or pulls, falling objects.)

2. **How does showing Jesus' love help others learn about Him?** (Helps others discover what the people who love Jesus are like. Helps them understand how much Jesus loves them.)

3. **How has someone shown Jesus' love to you and your family?**

4. **How can you show Jesus' love to someone else?**

Making Music

We can thank God for all things and in all circumstances because we know He is always with us.

Teacher Materials

Bible with bookmark at Ephesians 5:19,20; six identical clear water glasses; pitcher of water; spoon.

Prepare the Object Talk

Fill the glasses with water as shown in sketch.

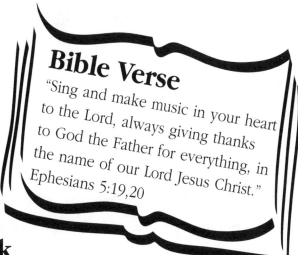

Bible Verse

"Sing and make music in your heart to the Lord, always giving thanks to God the Father for everything, in the name of our Lord Jesus Christ." Ephesians 5:19,20

Introduce the Object Talk

We all have times or situations that make us feel sad or happy. Because we know God is good and always with us, we can thank God for all things. Let's try a fun way to give thanks to God.

Present the Object Talk

1. Demonstrate how to play musical notes by gently tapping the glasses with the spoon. Point out to the children that different amounts of water in glasses cause different notes. (Optional: Invite volunteers to experiment with tapping the glasses.)

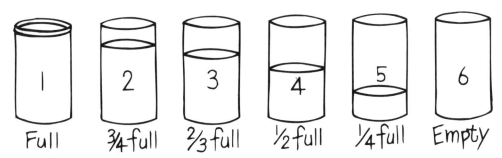

2. It's fun to make up our own music with these glasses. Listen to Ephesians 5:19,20 to see what it says about music. Read verses aloud. **Making music in our heart means we're so glad and thankful that our prayers to God are like songs.**

Many of the songs we sing in church are prayers of thankfulness and praise to God.

3. Choose a phrase from the verses such as "giving thanks to God the Father" or "Sing and make music in your heart" and tap the glasses as you say or sing the words. Invite children to say or sing the words with you. (Optional: Invite several children to tap the glasses for these or other phrases from the verses.)

Bible Verse

"Sing and make music in your heart to the Lord, always giving thanks to God the Father for everything, in the name of our Lord Jesus Christ." Ephesians 5:19,20

Conclude

Lead children in a prayer of thanks to God.

Discussion Questions

1. What are some ways of giving thanks to God? (Saying prayers. Writing prayers.)

2. What are some things you are thankful for?

3. When might you and your family give thanks to God at home?

Get Ready!

God gets us ready to do good things for Him.

Teacher Materials

Bible with bookmark at Philippians 2:13, one or more of the following diagrams or maps: blueprints, highway map, city street map, topographical or trail map, ocean depth chart, map of school, map of museum or mall.

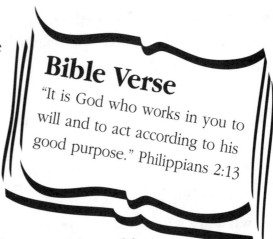

Bible Verse

"It is God who works in you to will and to act according to his good purpose." Philippians 2:13

Introduce the Object Talk

We've all done things to get ready for an important event like a birthday party or a Christmas celebration. God wants us to get ready to do the good things He wants us to do, too. Look at these maps and diagrams and think about how they help you prepare for something.

Present the Object Talk

One at a time, show each kind of map or diagram you have brought. **What would this (map) help you get ready for? What kind of information do you learn from this (diagram)? Why is the information on here important? What might happen if you didn't have this map or diagram?** (Might get lost. Wouldn't know how long trip would take. Couldn't plan how to get to the place we're going.)

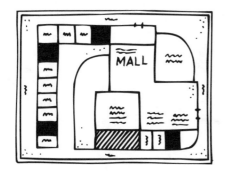

Conclude

Before we take a trip or build a building, it's important to get ready so that we can do a good job. **Who helps us get ready to do the good things God wants us to do?** Read Philippians 2:13 aloud. **This verse tells us that we don't have to try to obey God by ourselves. He promises to help us love and obey Him.** Pray, thanking God that He is with us to help us do good.

Bible Verse

"It is God who works in you to will and to act according to his good purpose." Philippians 2:13

Discussion Questions

1. **What are some other things kids your age need to get ready for?** (Spelling test. Piano recital. Basketball game.) **How do you get ready for them?** (Practice. Ask God's help.)

2. **What are some of the ways we can get ready to do the good things God wants us to do?** (Learn about God. Read the Bible. Talk to God.)

3. **What's something good you think God might want you to do?** (Be honest. Treat others fairly.)

What Do You Need?

No matter what we need, God helps and cares for us.

Teacher Materials

Bible with bookmark at Philippians 4:19, picture or photo of a baby (or a baby doll), apple, sharp object.

Bible Verse

"My God will meet all your needs according to his glorious riches in Christ Jesus." Philippians 4:19

Introduce the Object Talk

No matter how young or old we are and no matter what we need, God says He will give us what we need. Sometimes it seems like we don't get the things we need. Let's talk about why we might feel that way and discover if it's really true.

Present the Object Talk

1. Show picture or photo of baby, or pass around doll, letting volunteers pantomime ways of caring for a baby. **What are some of the ways people care for babies? How do babies get the things they need? Someone who cares for a baby will make sure to give the baby things like food, water, milk, hugs and toys to play with.**

2. Listen to this verse about the things we need. Read Philippians 4:19 aloud. **What does this verse say God does?** (God gives us the good things we need.)

3. The Bible tells us to ask God for the things we need. But sometimes we ask God for something and we don't get it. Because God loves us so much, He might say no to our request because He knows that what we've asked for isn't good for us. Show sharp object, keeping out of children's reach. **If a baby wants to play with a (knife), how do people protect the baby?**

4. Other times when we ask God for something, His answer is to wait. Show apple. **Why is an apple good for you to eat? Why is an apple not good for a baby to eat?** (Baby might choke on apple pieces.) **Just as babies have to wait until they are older to eat apples, God knows we have to wait for some things.**

Bible Verse
"My God will meet all your needs according to his glorious riches in Christ Jesus."
Philippians 4:19

Conclude

When we pray and ask God to give us the things we need, we know that His answers are always best. Lead children in prayer, thanking God for meeting our needs.

Discussion Questions

1. **What are some of the things God provides for us?** (People to care for us. Food to eat. Friends.)

2. **How do people show that they are depending on God to give them what they need?** (Ask God for needs. Don't complain about things they want but don't have.)

3. **What's something you are thankful God has given to you?**

Helicopter Project

When we show love for God by working together, good things can be accomplished.

Teacher Materials

Bible with bookmark at Colossians 3:23, four ¾×6-inch (1.9×15-cm) paper strips, scissors, ruler, paper clips; optional—additional materials.

Bible Verse

"Whatever you do, work at it with all your heart, as working for the Lord, not for men." Colossians 3:23

Introduce the Object Talk

Whenever there is a big or small project to be done, it helps to have more than one good worker. God wants us to do good work to show our love for Him. Today we'll work together to make paper helicopters. Each of you will have a part to do.

Present the Object Talk

1. Select four volunteers. Volunteers stand in single-file line at a table. Give first volunteer the paper strips, scissors and ruler. Hand third volunteer the paper clips.

2. First volunteer cuts a 2-inch (5-cm) slit in the top of each paper strip (see sketch a). Second volunteer folds the lower corners of each strip to a point (see sketch b). Third volunteer attaches a paper clip to the folded part of the strip (see sketch c). Fourth volunteer folds one half of the cut portion of the strips in one direction and the other half in the opposite direction (see sketch d).

3. Volunteers fly helicopters by holding the paper clip and tossing the helicopters up in the air.

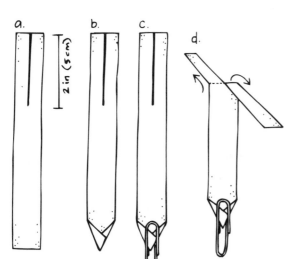

Small Group Option

Children form groups of four. Each group makes four helicopters.

Conclude

Because each person did his or her part, we were able to make helicopters. Why does Colossians 3:23 say it's important to do our best work? Read verse aloud. **A good way to show love for God is by working together with other people.** Ask God's help in working with others to do the good things God wants us to do.

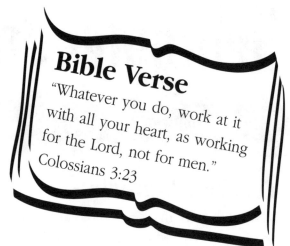

Bible Verse

"Whatever you do, work at it with all your heart, as working for the Lord, not for men."
Colossians 3:23

Discussion Questions

1. **What might have happened if someone didn't do careful work in making the helicopter?**

2. **What are some times kids need to do their best job when working with others to complete a project?** (School projects. Sports teams.)

3. **What are some examples of ways in which people who live together need to work together?** (Cleaning up after dinner. Decorating a Christmas tree. Cleaning the yard.)

4. **What's one way you can help someone else by doing your best work?**

Watch and Wait

God always answers prayer—sometimes in ways we don't expect.

Teacher Materials

Bible with bookmark at Colossians 4:2, newspapers, several paper plates, glue, salt in a shaker, paintbrush, watercolor paint, container of water.

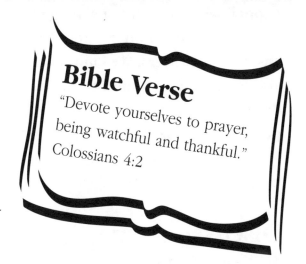

Bible Verse
"Devote yourselves to prayer, being watchful and thankful." Colossians 4:2

Prepare the Object Talk

Make a practice design, following the directions below.

Introduce the Object Talk

Sometimes when something takes a long time to happen, we get tired of waiting and watching for it to happen. When we pray to God, we need to wait and watch to see Him answer our prayers. Watch to see what happens in this experiment.

Present the Object Talk

1. Cover table or floor with newspapers. Squeeze glue onto a paper plate, creating a design of thick lines that intersect.

2. Immediately pour salt over the lines, making sure to cover the glue completely. Shake excess salt onto glue. Saturate paintbrush with water so that it is very wet.

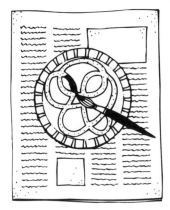

Then dab watercolor paint onto one of the lines, holding the brush at one place. The color will move along the lines as the salt absorbs the water in the paint. Encourage children to keep watching to see what happens to the paint.

3. After the color has stopped spreading, rinse the brush in water and apply another color of paint at a different place. The two paints will mix at the point where they meet. **What did you expect would happen? What did happen?**

Small Group Option

Provide materials for children to create their own designs.

Bible Verse

"Devote yourselves to prayer, being watchful and thankful." Colossians 4:2

Conclude

Just as we watched to see what would happen with the paint, it's up to us to keep watching to find out how God will answer our prayers. We know God will always keep His promise to answer our prayers. Read Colossians 4:2 aloud. **When we devote ourselves to prayer, we never give up praying and looking to see how God will answer our prayers. Sometimes God answers our prayers in ways we don't expect.** Lead children in prayer, thanking God for always hearing and answering our prayers.

Discussion Questions

1. **What are some things kids your age often talk to God about?** (When help is needed to do something. To thank Him for having something good or for something good happening.)

2. **Why might God answer a prayer by saying "no" or "later"?** (God knows what's best for us.)

3. **In what way has God answered a prayer for you or someone in your family?**

4. **What's something you want to talk to God about?**

Paper Challenge

Teacher Materials

Bible with 1 Thessalonians 5:14 marked with a bookmark, one or more of these materials: toilet paper, crepe-paper strip, yarn, curling ribbon, narrow fabric strip.

Bible Verse

"Encourage the timid, help the weak, be patient with everyone." 1 Thessalonians 5:14

Introduce the Object Talk

God tells us in His Word that He wants us to help people who are weak. Watch to see what is weak in this experiment and what makes the weak item become strong.

Present the Object Talk

1. Invite a volunteer to come forward. Ask the volunteer to hold wrists together in front of him- or herself as you wrap one strand of toilet paper around the wrists. Challenge the volunteer to break free.

2. Repeat several times, each time adding one or two strands of paper before the volunteer tries to break free. Comment, **One or two strands of paper are weak and we can break them easily. The more strands of paper we add, the stronger the paper becomes.** Repeat with other volunteers and/or materials.

Conclude

When we try to trust in God by ourselves, it's like we are as weak as one strand of paper. We might find it hard to do what God says. But when others help us and encourage us, it's easier to trust God. We are stronger together—just as the papers were stronger when they were put together. Count the ways this verse says we can help others. Read 1 Thessalonians 5:14 aloud. Pray, asking God to show children ways of helping others to trust Him.

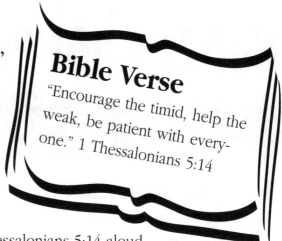

Bible Verse

"Encourage the timid, help the weak, be patient with everyone." 1 Thessalonians 5:14

Discussion Questions

1. **When might it be hard for a kid to do what God wants? How could a friend help him or her to obey?** (Pray for him or her. Say helpful words to him or her.)

2. **What's something you know God wants you to do?** (Be honest. Stand up for someone who needs help.) **How could you also help a friend obey God in that way?**

3. **Who has helped you learn about God and trust in Him?**

Ask God!

Teacher Materials

Bible with bookmark at 1 Thessalonians 5:17,18; flashlight with batteries; plant; votive candle; match; large wide-mouthed jar; snack for each child.

Bible Verse

"Pray continually; give thanks in all circumstances."
1 Thessalonians 5:17,18

Introduce the Object Talk

If we want to get to know God and obey Him, we need to talk to Him every day. Let's look at these objects and talk about what they need in order to work.

Present the Object Talk

1. Show flashlight and ask children to tell what it needs to work (batteries). **What are some other items which need batteries in order to work?** (CD player, hand-held video games, toys, etc.)

2. Show plant and ask children to tell what it needs to grow (water, sunlight). **What are some other things which need water and sunlight to grow?** (Trees, flowers, etc.)

3. Light candle. **What does this candle need to burn?** (Oxygen.) Cover candle with jar and watch to see the candle flame go out. Repeat experiment, inviting children to count how long it takes for the flame to go out.

4. What do you need to do every day to live and grow? (Eat food. Drink water. Breathe air.) Serve snack to each child.

Conclude

We've talked about what all these items need. What does 1 Thessalonians 5:17,18 say we need to do? Read verses aloud. **Sometimes we only think about praying to God when we have a problem or need something. But when does 1 Thessalonians 5:17,18 say we should pray? Talking to God every day about what we are doing and the choices we are making helps us love and obey Him.** Lead children in prayer, thanking Him that we can talk to Him.

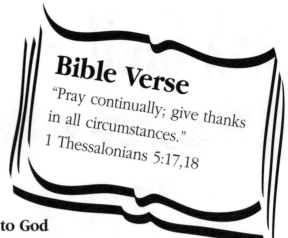

Bible Verse
"Pray continually; give thanks in all circumstances."
1 Thessalonians 5:17,18

Discussion Questions

1. When can you talk to God?

2. What are some things a kid your age could tell God about school?

3. Who might help you remember to pray?

4. What's something you'd like to thank God for right now?

Gifts to Grow By

God can do great things with our gifts to Him.

Teacher Materials
Bible with bookmark at 1 Timothy 6:18, popcorn kernels, measuring cup, popcorn maker, two bowls, napkins; optional—salt.

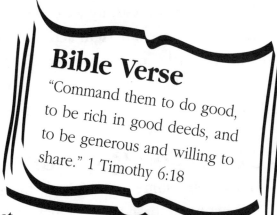

Bible Verse
"Command them to do good, to be rich in good deeds, and to be generous and willing to share." 1 Timothy 6:18

Introduce the Object Talk
Our gifts to God can be used by Him in many ways. Even small gifts of love and time can make a big difference. Let's look at something that starts out small and grows to be big!

Present the Object Talk

1. Pour popcorn kernels into measuring cup until they measure half a cup (or the measurement appropriate for your popcorn maker). Ask a volunteer to look at the measuring cup and tell how much corn is in the cup.

2. What happens to these popcorn kernels when they are heated? (They pop. They get bigger.) Invite children to tell how much corn they think will be popped from the half cup of kernels.

3. Pop popcorn and measure it. (Optional: Ask Discussion Questions while waiting for kernels to pop.) Children compare their predictions with the actual number of cups of popped corn.

4. Serve popcorn to children. (Optional: Children sprinkle salt on popcorn.)

Conclude

Sometimes we think our gifts to God are small and won't make much of a difference. But even our small gifts can be used by God in great ways. Listen to 1 Timothy 6:18 to find out some ways we can give to God. Read verse aloud. What does this verse say we can give to others? How are our right actions a gift to God? (Our right actions show love for God and help others learn about Him.) Lead children in prayer, asking God to show us ways to give to Him and to others.

Bible Verse

"Command them to do good, to be rich in good deeds, and to be generous and willing to share." 1 Timothy 6:18

Discussion Questions

1. **What are some other things that start out small and get bigger?** (Cookies, until they're baked. Babies, until they grow to be adults. Plant and tree seeds, until they're planted and watered.)

2. **In what ways might kids your age give to God?** (Give time to help others. Donate possessions we have that are needed by others.) Tell children about ways the people in your church give to others to show love for God.

3. **What is one way you can give to God?**

More Than Enough!

God's wisdom helps us know what's best to do.

Teacher Materials

Bible with bookmark at James 1:5, table, one or more of the following: room freshener spray; electric fan with several settings; pitcher of water, small cup and plastic dishpan; snack divided into both bite-size and larger portions.

Bible Verse

"If any of you lacks wisdom, he should ask God, who gives generously to all without finding fault, and it will be given to him." James 1:5

Introduce the Object Talk

We're talking today about wisdom—knowing what's best to do and say. God promises to give us wisdom if we ask Him. Watch what I do to discover a word that describes the way in which God gives us wisdom.

Present the Object Talk

1. One at a time complete one or more of these demonstrations to illustrate what it means to do something generously: *(a)* Ask children what they smell as you first

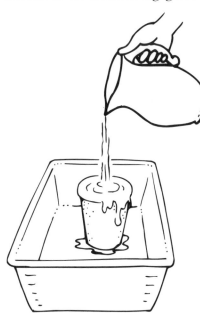

spray a small amount of room freshener and then spray a larger amount. *(b)* Ask children what they feel as you first turn on fan at lowest speed and then turn fan to highest speed. *(c)* Ask children what they see as you first pour a tiny amount of water into cup and then pour water into cup until it overflows into the dishpan. *(d)* Ask children what they taste as you first serve bite-size portions of snack to children and then serve larger portions to children.

2. Of the actions I just did, which one(s) would you describe as generous? Which one(s) were not? Why? How do you know if someone is generous or not?

Conclude

Listen to what the Bible says about God's promise of wisdom. Read James 1:5 aloud. **What should we do if we need wisdom, being able to understand what happens and know the right thing to do?** Pray, asking God for wisdom and thanking Him for giving wisdom generously.

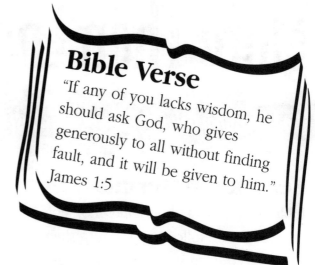

Bible Verse

"If any of you lacks wisdom, he should ask God, who gives generously to all without finding fault, and it will be given to him."
James 1:5

Discussion Questions

1. **Who are some wise people you know? What do you think makes them wise?**

2. **When is a time a kid your age needs to be wise?** (To understand what God want us to do.) **Why?**

3. **Why can we be sure God will give us wisdom if we ask for it?** (God's Word tells us.)

4. **How can you be wise today?** (Follow God's Word. Listen to our parents.)

Salt Surprise

Keep on telling about God your whole life, looking for ways in every situation to share God's love with others.

Teacher Materials

Bible with bookmark at 1 Peter 3:15, plastic wrap, bowl, tape, salt, measuring spoon, metal pan with lid.

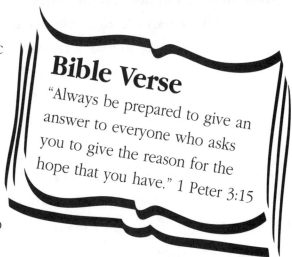

Bible Verse

"Always be prepared to give an answer to everyone who asks you to give the reason for the hope that you have." 1 Peter 3:15

Prepare the Object Talk

Tightly stretch a piece of plastic wrap over the bowl, taping it securely. Practice Step 1 below to make sure the plastic wrap is on tight enough.

Introduce the Object Talk

It's important for God's followers to keep telling others about Him, giving reasons why we believe in and love God. See if you can figure out the reason, or explanation, for why something in this experiment moves without our touching it.

Present the Object Talk

1. Sprinkle one teaspoon of salt evenly onto the plastic. Then invite a volunteer to stand several feet (meters) from the bowl and bang the lid onto the pan at the level of the top of the bowl. The salt will move on the plastic.

2. As time permits, invite additional volunteers to take a turn banging the pan. Ask volunteers to tell reasons why they think the salt moves. Acknowledge each child's idea.

3. We've talked about some ideas about why the salt moves. Listen to the reason, or explanation, according to scientists: We can't see sounds, but

they are vibrations in the air, so sounds make the air move. These vibrations in the air make the plastic move, or vibrate, so that the salt moves.

Bible Verse

"Always be prepared to give an answer to everyone who asks you to give the reason for the hope that you have." 1 Peter 3:15

Conclude

Hearing a reason for why something is true helps us understand it better. Listen to 1 Peter 3:15 to find what God wants us to be ready to give a reason for. Read verse aloud. **The hope we have is our belief in God and His love and forgiveness for us. This verse reminds us to tell others about what we believe.** Lead children in prayer, asking His help in telling others about His love.

Discussion Questions

1. **What do you know about God that others should know? about Jesus?**

2. **Who has told you about Jesus and helped you learn about reasons to love and obey Him?**

3. **What are things kids your age can do to learn about Jesus?** (Read the Bible. Listen to stories from the Bible. Ask parents or teachers to help you understand what verses from the Bible mean.)

Special Love

The same God who made the world and us, shows His love to all who are His children.

Teacher Materials

Bible with bookmark at 1 John 3:1.

Materials for Children

Several leaves from a variety of trees (small rocks, potatoes or other nature items may be substituted); optional—a leaf (or other nature item) for each child.

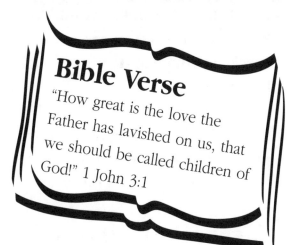

Bible Verse

"How great is the love the Father has lavished on us, that we should be called children of God!" 1 John 3:1

Introduce the Object Talk

When God made the world, He did many things to show His love for us. One thing God did was make each thing He created special. Try to figure out what is special about the leaf I give you.

Present the Object Talk

1. Select six to eight volunteers and give each volunteer a leaf. Allow volunteers a short time to examine leaves. **What do you notice about the size of your leaf? its color? How does your leaf feel?** Volunteers briefly compare leaves. **Look carefully at your leaf, so you can find your leaf again when they're all mixed up.**

2. Collect leaves (include extra leaves) and group them together on table or floor. Volunteers try to find their leaves. **How hard was it to find your leaf? What helped you find your leaf?** Volunteers answer. **The more you knew about your leaf, the easier it was to find it.**

Small Group Option

All children are given leaves and participate.

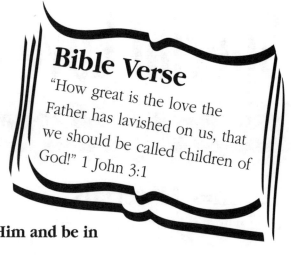

Bible Verse

"How great is the love the Father has lavished on us, that we should be called children of God!" 1 John 3:1

Conclude

Because God made each of us, He knows us and loves us. No matter how many people there are in the world, God knows and loves each person. We are so special to Him that He wants us to love Him and be in His family.

Read (or ask a volunteer to read) 1 John 3:1 aloud. **The word "lavish" means to give more than is needed. This verse reminds us of God's love. The reason God made the world and us is to show love.** Pray, thanking God for His love and for the special way in which He made the world and us.

Discussion Questions

1. **What are some other things in creation that look similar but are really different from each other?** (Snowflakes. Stars.)

2. **What are some ways God made each person unique?** (Our fingerprints. Our voices. Our smiles.)

3. **What are some ways God has shown love to you and your family?**

Link Up!

Teacher Materials

Bible with bookmark at 1 John 4:19, pencils, 1×6-inch (2.5×15-cm) strips of paper (several for each child), tape.

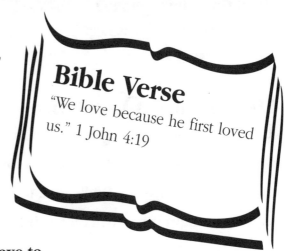

Bible Verse

"We love because he first loved us." 1 John 4:19

Introduce the Object Talk

Our love and caring for others begins with God's love for us. Let's help each other make a paper chain that shows some of the people we can show God's love to.

Present the Object Talk

1. Print the name of one child on your own paper strip and say the name aloud. Tape the ends of the strip together, forming a link.

2. Ask for volunteers to suggest another child's name (or the name of a friend or family member) that begins with the last letter of the name you wrote. One volunteer writes one of the suggested names on a paper strip, inserts it through your link and tapes the ends together, forming a second link (see sketch).

3. Continue process, making paper chain as long as possible. Children may also make a paper chain with words of 1 John 4:19, repeating the verse until each child has added a word.

Conclude

When our names are linked together in this chain, it reminds us that we can show God's love to each other. Read 1 John 4:19 aloud. **What does 1 John 4:19 say about God? How does knowing about God's love help us?** Thank God for His love and ask His help in showing care to others.

Bible Verse
"We love because he first loved us." 1 John 4:19

Discussion Questions

1. What are some ways God has shown His love to us?

2. How has someone shown God's love to you?

3. How can you show God's love to others?

4. When might it be difficult to show God's love to someone?

Thematic Index

Bible (see God's Word)

Guidance from God

Help
For Others

From God

Love

For God

For Others

From God

Obedience

Power of God (see God's Nature)

Praise

Prayer

Salvation

Thanking God

Witnessing

Worship

Smart Resources for Your Children's Ministry

Sunday School Smart Pages
Edited by Wes and Sheryl Haystead
Training, inspiration, materials, quick solutions and more for teaching ages 2 through 12.
Reproducible.
Manual • ISBN 08307.15215

Sunday School Promo Pages
Wes and Sheryl Haystead
Resources and advice to recruit teachers, gain church support, increase attendance and more.
Reproducible.
Manual • ISBN 08307.15894

5th & 6th Grade Smart Pages
Wes Haystead and Tom Prinz
The most current information, tips and quick solutions for teaching 5th and 6th grades, plus parent education articles.
Reproducible.
Manual • ISBN 08307.18052

Nursery Smart Pages
Legal and safety guidelines, teacher's pages, parent pages, classroom activities, clip art, and much more!
Reproducible.
Manual • ISBN 08307.19067

VBS Smart Pages
Advice, answers and articles for a successful Vacation Bible School. Includes forms, records and clip art.
Reproducible.
Manual • ISBN 08307.16718

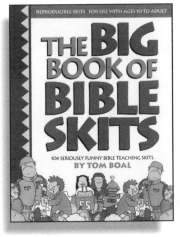

The Big Book of Bible Skits
Tom Boal
104 seriously funny Bible teaching skits. Includes discussion questions.
Reproducible.
Manual • ISBN 08307.19164

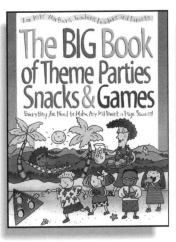

The Big Book of Theme Parties, Snacks & Games
Decorating ideas, snack recipes, wacky activities, games, clip art, and more for eight complete themes.
Reproducible.
Manual • ISBN 08307.18206

The Big Book of Bible Games
200 fun games that teach Bible concepts and life application.
Reproducible.
ISBN 08307.18214

Available from your Gospel Light supplier or call **1-800-4-GOSPEL.**